TUF
AS A BOILED OWL

The Civil War Letters of
Proctor Swallow 7th Vermont
Volunteer Regiment

Compiled By:
Kenena Hansen Spalding

Bloomington, IN

authorHOUSE™

Milton Keynes, UK

AuthorHouse™
1663 Liberty Drive, Suite 200
Bloomington, IN 47403
www.authorhouse.com
Phone: 1-800-839-8640

AuthorHouse™ UK Ltd.
500 Avebury Boulevard
Central Milton Keynes, MK9 2BE
www.authorhouse.co.uk
Phone: 08001974150

First published by AuthorHouse 5/17/2006

ISBN: 1-4259-1959-6 (sc)

Library of Congress Control Number: 2006903075

Printed in the United States of America
Bloomington, Indiana

This book is printed on acid-free paper.

In memory of Aunt Fanny and Aunt Helen

Who cared for the past to share with the future

CONTENTS

ONE
JOURNEYMAN FARMHAND

Proctor Swallow spent the summer of his twenty-second year as a hired man on a farm just across the Vermont State border in Whitehall, New York. He left that job in the fall and joined a threshing crew harvesting crops in the region. While aware of the events embroiling the country, he was more concerned with finances and getting cash money, always a need in an agrarian economy. He wrote to his friend Loomis Spalding, now the new husband of his sister Fanny, about possible options, local affairs, and his homesickness.

Whitehall
July 8th 61

Mr. Spalding

I take my pen in hand to fulfill my promise to write you I waited a week longer than I had intended to when I was at home Adams thought he might get some money in a few days but I did not see any sign of it money is awfull tight he says that he has not had twenty dollars at one time this summer I guess that he could raise money enough if he was going to some horse race but I dont know   Cheese is a tiptop article here   it is worth from four to five cnts per pound and you cant get money at that   it was very still times here   the week after I was at home two ruffians murdered a woman the 27ʰ   they have gone up three more arrest for robing a man of his watch they brok jail and fled   an officer attempts to arrest a fellow and was stabed   another was sent to the clay banks for stealing and (?) for getting drunk   give my best respects to your wife and children   hoping these lines will find all enjoying good health   I must bid you Adieu as my candle is just going out and ink to   grass is looking fine and the weather is very warm   good bye

Proctor Swallow
NB don't forget to write very soon

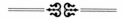

Whitehall
Sept 8ᵗʰ 1861

Friends at home

I have given up ever comeing to Vermont again and so I will write you a few lines   I am well now and hope these lines will find you all enjoying the same blessing   I have been comeing home for the last two months but I have not got there yet and I cant tell now when I shall come   I think not untill my ship comes in   I should wrote you before but I have been unwell and I wanted to see whether I lived or died   well I rather guess I am alive and have been smart as ever for the past week   I am not to work for Mr. Adams now   I am threshing with a machine now for a man by the name of Pratt   we thrash for every tenth or five dollars per day   if you was not so far off we would come and do your threshing but you live the wrong way we travell south   oats are very low   25 cts per bush and no money at that   Jeff Davis they say is dead   well I am not sorry but it is hard to wish a man dead   I have seen tough times by his doings but not so tough as some have   I have no desire to enlist   I understand that they are geting up a company in Poultney   they got up a company of 43 here but when they came to start they all carved out but six and one of them went no farther than Troy   I was ashamed of my last letter   I did not expect any answer but I was in a hurry and did not have much ink   come down home today on purpose to write and I am going to write more   I guess then you will be able to read

tell mother to keep on good terms with old Newton and quit smokeing and she may get that nice little place of his   tell bub to save his money to buy wood and if Julia is there give her my best respects I would like to see early   I never stayed away from home so long before   it is something over two months since I was at home   I suppose I see you at the State Fair if I should go   but the times are to rough   I dont think I could stand the press   I have been saveing a three sent piece a long time to pay postage on this letter and then I am broke   I think that famous calf of Jobs was no comparison to me this summer   I dont want you to be as long answering this letter as I was yours　　　I shall be down town again in about two weeks and should like to find something at the office　　　I intend to write every two weeks untill I come home when I get through threshing　　　I dont know but I shall go peddleing　　　cant tell now　　　I think I should make a good one　　　I hope you will not find room in your letter to say anything about money for there is but three cents in town and I have got that　　　but I shant have it long　　　I have to take shin plasters to buy my tobacco

well I am getting out of writeing timber and so I might as well bring my letter to a close　　　I want you to send me all the news you can get hold of　　　we have had a nice garden this summer we had cabbage six weeks ago　　beets　peas and everything that any boddy could ask for

I think the north has got more than they bargained for to whip the south　　　they may do it in time but they are very tough

Well I am done

write soon

　　　　　　　　　　　　　　　　Yours
　　　　　　　　　　　　　　Proctor Swallow

Whitehall
Sept 28 (1861)

*A good evening to you all   I arrived safe and sound
at Whitehall at forty minutes past four the day I
left Poultney   I will make you a harness or rather
have one made   I want you to write me what kind
of harnes   you want   I think that high ones is
the best for a double harness but as you want to
use it single some you can have which you like   I
have played out on threshing machienes   we got
140 bushel of oats which brought $35.00   paid
man and team $30.00   repairs $20.00   oil $2.00
express $2.00   leaving us a net profit of $19.00
but out of pocket we gave up the old machiene
and I am working out by the month   I want you to
write all about the fair as I have not heard a word
about it   tell me who had the fastest horse and
what kind of a time you had the 21ˢᵗ   give my
best respects to Julia and all others that should
trouble themselves to inquire   tell mother I have
not gone for a solger yet   I saw   A Smith 2ⁿᵈ out
here the other day   he had been out and was
going home before I was fairly up there   I guess
that I have wrote all that my sheet will allow*

Good By
Proctor Swallow

===❦===

Whitehall
Oct 26ᵗʰ 1861

Well   Loomis   I have concluded to write to you
again   I wrote to you in a few days after I was
at home and have got no answer yet   I wrote
you that would get you up a harnes and wished
you would tell me what kind of harnes you would
have high or low   I dont know as you got it

I want you to write to me or I shall get mad and
come home and then I guess your maple suggar
and pancakes will have to suffer   I am well and
tuff as a boiled Owl   we had two feet of snow
or less last Friday   by golly how cold my fingers
was

give my best wishes to mother and Fanny Harriet
and that old gentleman Albion   I have paid Dan
Ensign and more to he ows me about six shilllings
you need not tell him that I said anything to you
about it   I sent him some Brandy and made him
a pair martengells   I sent him a bill of the stuff
and told him he mite send the balance by mail   I
will bet he was mad when he got it   dont fail to
write soon and if you can pick up any news send
it along   good bye

P. Swallow

TWO
CAMP PHELPS

The Vermont State Legislature on November 16th, 1861, enacted a law authorizing Governor Frederick Holbrook to "recruit, organize, arm and equip" a regiment of infantry to serve for the State in the Army of the United States[1] for three years. Colonel George T. Roberts[2] was given command of the regiment. He was the manager of the West Rutland marble quarries and brother-in law to the principle owner General H. H. Baxter. Volney S. Fullam was Lt. Colonel and William C. Holbrook of Brattleboro, the governor's son, was named major. Charles Ruggles of Poultney was designated Captain of I Company and charged with filling its ranks with men from the village and surrounding areas. Proctor Swallow enlisted as one of the recruits on January 7, 1862.

The regiment rendezvoused at the Rutland Fairgrounds on February 4. Proctor Swallow spent his twenty-third birthday at the encampment renamed Camp Phelps in honor of Colonel John C. Phelps.[3] He stood five feet six inches tall and had brown hair, blue eyes and a dark complexion. He became a victim as the customary measles epidemic ran through the camp during the five cold snowy winter weeks they trained

7

there. The *Rutland Daily Herald*[4] reported on the Order of Exercises for a day at the camp.

5:30 a.m.	Reville
6:10 a.m.	Roll Call
6:15 a.m.	Surgeon's Call
7:00 a.m.	Breakfast
8:00 a.m.	Guard Mounting
9 – 11 a.m.	Company Drill
11:00- noon	Dinner
1 –3 p.m.	Company Drill
4:30 p.m.	Dress Parade
6:00 p.m.	Supper
9:30 p.m.	Roll Call
9:45 p.m.	Tattoo (at which time all lights are extinguished except in officers' tents).

On March 10, newly armed with Springfield rifles, the troops left their barracks and boarded a train in Rutland. They were cordially welcomed upon their arrival in New York City. The officers were entertained by The Sons of Vermont at a Fifth Avenue hotel with a levee in their honor. On March 14, the soldiers marched down to the East River docks and embarked on two steamers *The Premier* and *The Tamerlane*. Once on board, their sealed orders were delivered and opened. The voyage was just underway when the ships were detained for several days at Sandy Hook, New Jersey because of unfavorable weather conditions. After leaving this anchorage the two ships parted company and did not meet again until arriving at the destination.

During the long and arduous voyage the men were confined in close and poorly arranged quarters aboard the vessels. There was little to eat and much of the time water was rationed. They suffered terribly from seasickness. Adding to the sadness, Frank Price of I Company died from an accidental wounding during the passage. The men watched as his body, wrapped in a blanket with iron slugs tied to the feet, was slid over the side on a plank and buried at sea. After twenty-two days they finally arrived at Ship Island off the coast of Louisiana.[5]

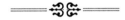

Camp Felps, 8 1862

Mr Spalding and all the rest of the folks   I write to you before I leave

I am in a great Hurry now and have no place to write but on the floor

bid mother and Fan and bub all good bye for me

tell Fan the lunch she sent me was first rate   we all had a good supper

good bye   I have sent a letter to Adams and if you can get anything   do so

P Swallow

Rutland,
March 9ᵗʰ, 1862

Well Friend Loomis

*according to my promice I will write you a few
lines   I am getting along finely*

I feel better today than I have in two weeks

*I wrote to Adams the other day and got an answer
to day   he says that he sent the money to me
and the other to you   perhaps it is at fair haven
now   he says that Ben Holcomb took a quart of it
I dont care if he did   I think it strange that I get
all Adams letters that dont contain anything and
none that do have anything in them   if you can get
that little that may be at the Fair haven depot well
and good but I dont think you will*

*there is a number of Poultney folks up here today
Ben Ward, Frank Jackson, and Dan Culver by
who I hear from*

*Mother, frs   well you must all be of good cheer as
I be and you will be all right   well I must bid you
all good   while I have room   I will write as soon
as I can.*

Yours,

P. Swallow

New York, March12, 62

According to my promice I write to you

we hve got to New York all right   we had a pleasant but a slow ride

I think I shall spend the rest of my days on the Banks of the Hudson   it is so pleasant   west Point is splendid place to

I think we shall sail tomorrow

well good bye and pleasant dreams to you all

I am well as ever   tuff as a boiled Owl

Yours

P. Swallow

THREE
SHIP ISLAND

After the long twenty-two day voyage, the *Premier* and the *Tamerlane* arrived at Ship Island, Louisiana on April 5, 1862. The men were not allowed to disembark until two days later on April 7th. The Seventh Regiment was assigned to General Butler's New England Division and almost immediately quarreling began between some of the officers and General Ben Butler. Against orders, the Vermonters insisted on bringing all their equipment ashore.[6] He fumed that this caused a delay in leaving the ships.

Ship Island in the Gulf of Mexico was strategically located a few miles offshore from Mobile Bay and about seventy-miles from the entrance to the Mississippi River. It was a narrow desolate place about seven miles long covered with snow-white sand dunes and marsh grass. The only other vegetation was a pine grove at the northeast end that provided wood for cooking fires. The original mission of the 14,000 men gathered there was to capture New Orleans, the largest city in the Confederacy. However, it surrendered to Admiral David G. Farragut on April 24th   General Butler was then appointed Military Governor of Louisiana and brought his division upriver as an army of occupation. The

Seventh Regiment was dispatched to Carrollton about six miles north of New Orleans and placed in General Phelps Brigade.[7]

May 4ᵗʰ 1862
Ship Island

Friend Loomis

I will now begin an other letter the last I think I shall write from here

part of our Regt has gone somewhere I dont know where and we shall follow them soon I think

of the conditshions of things here I can say nothing   I mean the troops and their movements and numbers

my health is good and I hope when I hear from you to hear the same of you   I have written 3 letters before   think you have got one by this time

we have a daily paper printed here   its size is 7 by 9

the weather is not as warm as I expected to find it is warm in the day time and cool nights so we wear overcoats

I cant get much news about war   what little I do get is from New Orleans way   I think seseshion is about gone up

I think if we was on main land we find hotter weather   the sea breese here makes it cool

I am in hopes to eat with you thanksgiving with you I would like to be there to get some strawberry short cake but I guess I shant this year

we have pleasant weather most of the time   when we are not on duty we go hunting or fishing   the game consists of sea gulls gnimia negroes and crocodiles   we caught one of the latter the other day four feet long   it was a young one

there is a machine shop with a steam engine in it here and a rail road that goes by hand

I suppose you are ploughing now wish I was to but never mind   twenty dols per month   no lost time   getting rich as blazes and black as a nigger besides   being some what wiser than I was

we are haveing better fare here than we did on the ship   our rations consist of pork ham beef potatoes beans rice bakers bread hard crackers tea coffee suggar and molasses more than any man can eat   there is bread and meat enough wasted here to feed one Regiment   I have had no fresh meat but once since we came here and that was a lobster that I caught while fishing and roasted

I suppose that mother is still on good terms with Newton   I want when you write that you should send all the news and send me the Tribune   I will send you an order for my allotted pay   pay the note you let Rod have and do as you like with the rest   that is if you get the money on it   good bye

Yours truly,

P.Swallow

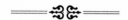

Ship Island,
May 12ᵗʰ 1862

Loomis

there is a vesel going to leave here today and I will send you a few lines by her   I mailed a letter a few days since but dont know how soon it will reach you if at all

I am well as usual   hope you are all the same at home

we have   I got a healthy place here much better than it would be on main land

they don't allow us to say any thing about the movements of troops here or anything of that kind   I get but little war news here   we do get is from New Orleans which I understand is in our possession

*tell Mother I am comeing home Christmas I think
we shall get Reb by that time where he cant
wigle*

*send me the Tribune once in awhile   we have a
daily paper here but it is no larger than this sheet
and not much news in it at that*

*had green peas here two weeks ago also ripe
plumbs   they came from New Orleans or some
where up that way   in my last letter I sent you
an order for Twenty Dollars   I wrote to you when
we first came on to the Island but I have heard
that the mail did not leave in two weeks after   if
so you have not got any of my letters yet*

*Tell Fanny I want her to bake me a berry shortcake
and put it in a letter and send to me*

*the weather begins to grow warm here   it is like
August in Vermont   I feel sorry for you farmers
who have to mow and sweat for $15 a month come
down to dixie get your little $20   and found
tobacco is cheap only $1.50 per pound cheese 30
cts   butter 62 cts*

*pay day has come but no pay   well if we get it we
wont spend it   they are as good as All Hyde was
keep a mans wages and not let squander them*

*we dont find as many Oranges and other fruit
here as we thought to when we left Rutland*

*I have heard that it was reported in Vt that we
were wrecked and all drowned   but I dont believe*

we was   if you get any of my letters answer them
right off and send all the news you can get hold
of   I would like to see some corn and oats growing
we have not got a spear of grays on the job   I
found a bean that had grown about six inches   it
made me think of home   there is night hawks
here and frogs   the evenings here are genorary
pleasant like a pleasant evening in old Vermont
well I guess I have wrote as much as you will care
about hearing this time so good bye

Direct to Proctor Swallow

Co. I 7th   git Reg, Vol

Gen. Phelps Brigade

Ship Island, Miss

Your Respectfully,

P. Swallow

If you get the money an the order send me a dollar
worth of stamps   they are very scarce here

FOUR
BATON ROUGE

Admiral Farragut continued up the Mississippi River and the capital city of Baton Rouge fell as quickly as New Orleans. "Proceed to Vicksburg... take the town or have it burned at all hazards" was the next order given to Admiral Farragut and General Thomas Williams by General Butler on the 16th of June. He further ordered that a regiment or two be sent "to cut off the neck of land beyond Vicksburg, by means of a trench across." He directed that the trench be made "about four feet deep and five feet wide. The river will do the rest for us." Success would have made the capture of the city unnecessary, by nullifying the guns of the Confederate fortress along the river bank.

The Seventh Regiment boarded the *Ceres* on June 20th to participate in this expedition. They took ten days rations, some cooking utensils, a week's supply of medical stores and no other equipment. As they approached Grand Gulf an infantry force under Lt. Col. Fullam was landed with orders to approach the village from the rear. They found most of the enemy gone. The transports continued on to Vicksburg and arrived there on June 25. The bombardment of the Confederate works began the next day and the men were set to work

digging the canal. Blacks from nearby plantations were brought in to help.

The canal quickly became known as "Butler's
Ditch".   As the summer heat increased, sickness raged throughout the camp. Malaria spread
by mosquitoes from the lowlands and dysentery
from the stagnant pools near the campsites were
rampant. There was a lack of wholesome food:
no vegetables, scarcely any fresh meat, and poor
quality rations. The impure and muddy waters of
the Mississippi River were all they had to use for
drinking and cooking. There was a dearth of suit-
able medicines and what they had brought was
exhausted quickly. The navy tried to share but
there was never enough. The men were housed in
confined quarters aboard the ship because they
had no tents. As the increasing number of sick
required all the room on board, those fit for duty
were ordered ashore to sleep on the ground. By
the time the project was abandoned, only 100 of
the 750 men who had gone up to Vicksburg were
fit for duty. Surgeon Enoch Blanchard of Lyndon
described the departure: "By some means, I
scarcely know how, we got 300 sick and helpless
men over to the levee opposite Vicksburg, without
tents or blankets and without food or medicines.
Just at night it began to rain in a drizzling sort of
way. I managed to get a limited supply of crackers and teas and spent the night wading through
the mud distributing these articles of nourish-
ment."[8]

Baton Rouge
Louisiana
June 12th '62

*Why in thunder dont you write to a fellow   I have
writen half a bushel of letter to you and have not
received one   I am getting furious not hear a
word after being here three months   if you dont
intend to write just come down and let a fellow
know it   well I suppose you do write but   I dont
get any letters   I shant never write again until I
hear from you   you neednent expect much this
time   wont get it if you do*

*we got marching orders the 6th and left Camp
Parrifet the 10th and come here   we are about 130
miles above New Orleans   we had a pleasant ride
up the River and we are in a perfect paradise now
we occupy the Arsenal Buildings and grounds
the buildings are brick three stories high and airy
we have good well water   the first good water we
have had since we left N.York   the grounds are
covered with green grass and shade trees and is
on a rise of ground l00 feet above the River   the
only high ground I have seen since we left the NY
the land on both sides of the river between here
and our former camp is covered with suggar cane
and is several feet lower than the water   the Levee
prevents the water from flooding the land   I saw
some splendid places while coming here…..a large
Plantation with suggar houses and negroes huts
resembles a small city   busifiness is dull here*

most of the publick Buildings are closed   a large
portion of the inhabitants have left the place

the weather is pleasant and warm   I wear woolen
drawers and shirt and do not feel the heat as
much as I do in Vermont sometimes

I had intended to visit New Orleans before we left
our old camp but could not get away   there is
several men in our Regt. that deserted the Rebbels
I am glad we are going from N.O wont be so apt to
get the yellow fever and black jack   I think our
stay here is not very long but I dont know

I suppose that while I am lying in the shade you
are hoeing   Corn and Potatoes in the hot sun   poor
fellow   I feel sorry for you   hadent you better
enlist   they are paying $20 per month board and
clothes included   I suppose you dont have any
taxes to pay this year   is it hard times in Vermont
this season and what is labor worth say a smart
chap like myself   how does your grass and other
crops look and what is cheese worth   who is
working for you this summer   I shall be obliged
to send this letter stampless for the simple reason
that I have not got any stamps   I dont think
theres one in the Regt nor have we any money
the paymaster was around but had not begun to
pay the men off   I dont know how soon we shall
get our pay now   in one of my letters I asked you
to send me a few stamps but not knowing if you
got it I will ask you again to send me a few and
trust until you get your pay   what do you think
of that   dont send a great many for I may get kill
and they would be of no use to me $20 a month

and cant pay postage on your letters since I came to La.   I have been healthier than I have since I left Poultney for Rutland   I have not got well of my measels   I took cold when I left Rutland and they left me with a bad cough   I did not know but I was done for one spel   but since we got on earth I have got over it   I think I was never better and hope to continue   so I think I shal be home in a day or two

I dont as I have anything more to write now but I want you to write as you can afford to rather hard to have to pay postage both ways but if you will give me the stamps I will pay as well as anybody   I dont know as I have mentioned one of your names but if I serve you all alike there will be no chance to grumble   hopeing these lines will find you all enjoying good health   I will bid you good bye

From your humble servant

Proctor Swallow

L.C. Spalding   PS   you may direct your letter to me Co. G 7th Vt Regt New Orleans   Louisiana

I have you direct to NO because I dont know how soon we shall leave here and I should get a letter directed there as soon as anywhere

Yours,   P.Swallow

Butenong, La
June 13th 62

Loomis

I have had the good fortune to get a stamp by giving 15cts for it   we have a profitable way of getting money here   our suttler did not come with us   before we left I bought a lot of tobacco and sold what cost 28 cts for 15 in cash and gave it for a stamp so I will write a little more and get as near the value of it as I can   I have got nothing in particular to write   we drill from five til six A M and the same in the evening leaving us 11 hours to lounge   some are playing cards   pitching quarters and the balance lying in the shade   we have a nice bathing house   a swing and a bowling aley   I dont like as well as I did the old Gen   has ordered us to drill with knapsacks one hour in the evening[9]   we went out through the citty   the dust is ½ inches deep and oh dear how dirty we got yesturday   we drilled in the yard some of us thought to play roots on the Col by taking our over coats and other clothes out   but we could not get the start of him on a mean trick   he made us go through with inspection of knapsacks   all of us that did not have our clothes with us have to drill with them two hours extra today   I must close now the mail leaves in a few moments

Good bye

Yours,

P. Swallow

Baton Rouge
June 15th, 1862

Friends at home,

Being in good spirits I will commence another letter although I thought when I wrote my last that I would I would not write again until I hear from you it is against the regulations to let the Soldiers out of the camp ground but the Col yesterday let six of the most steady and reliable men go out into the citty of course I was one of the six we had a fine time although there is not as much to atract my attention as in New York or Troy there is a states Prison here that covers several acres of ground a large insane assylam it is a large nice building that with the State house is the only nice Building in the citty there is a Regt of men quartered in the State House it is a splendid building is of brick with a finish that resembles marble the interior is finished of a very nice with the floors all carpeted a marble statue of Washington in the center of the floor there is also a beautiful yard with nice walks flower beds and fish Ponds it is on the bank of the River and from the upper story you can view the country for many miles along the river the most of the Buildings are old wooden things there is a few deacent brick buildings and not but a few are on the whole it is a rather slim afair for the capital of the State we shall without doubt leave here in a few days when I get somewhere and get seteled I will finish my letter so adieu for the present

Yours, P. Swallow

June 17ʰ, 1862

Loomis,

*I received your letter of May 10 today   was very
happy to hear from you and to hear that you was
all well   it is the first I have heard from you   I
began to think you was never going to write   I
would rather have got the letter than $10.00 in
gold   Your Uncle Lartion is a hard nut I guess but
then I think if he would come and live with me I
could make a steady man of him   but as he grows
older he may get wiser   I think I do   I went with
50 men up the River yesterday   we supposed we
going up to Vicksburgh to shoot some Rebbels but
when we got 60 miles up the River they set us to
loading wood   we worked some and some we
dident   it took 24 hours to load 40 cord   I think
a soldier is the lazyest man on earth   I think we
shall go up the River in a day or two   well I think
I will bid you good bye for the present*

*Direct as usual until further orders to New
Orleans*

Yours,

P. Swallow

On Board Steamer Ceres
June 21ˢᵗ, 1862

*Left Baton Rouge 19ᵗʰ proseded up the stream 5
miles   took on a supply of coal   June 20ᵗʰ went 5
miles farther and landed on a Plantation   found
plenty of Fowls Hogs Sheep & Cattle   they
had to suffer   we lived fast here for awhile   I
think the boys brought away 5 bins of suggar
there was 1000 Bbls suggar and molasses   got
underway last night   are 60 miles from B R fleet
is 8 steamers loaded with Inft and two Batterys
Capn Faraguets Flag Ship and a few gun Boats
breakfast is ready   we are living well nowadays
some Wars in the Pudding but thats nothing get
inside it*

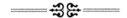

Steamer Ceres
June 22ⁿᵈ 1862

*We are 125 miles from B R   at sun set the Flag
Ship run aground   worked all night have not got
her off yet   get but little sleep   the musquitoes
are so thick they tore my blanket up trying to get
at me   they are large as yearlings   it must be
about Strawberry in Vermont   eat some for me
tell Mother I have had to stop chewing tobacco on
account of sore mouth   ask her is she dont feel
sorry for me*

Steamer Ceres
June 23ʳᵈ 1862

We got our Flag Ship off the bar at 9 oclock AM and run til 3 PM   things looked suspicious[10] landed two Regts one Battery   returned at 12 PM saw nothing   a reckless boy was drowned while Bathing got under the wheel   his Boddy was not recovered   the weather is very warm   yesterday hottest I have seen

Steamer Ceres
June 24ᵗʰ 1862

We are within a few miles of Grand Gulf   the Rebbels have a large force and are well fortyfied our gun boats have gone up the River   we have come up a chanel to attact them in the rear   it is the first time we have loaded our guns for a fight we are going to land soon

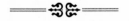

Steamer Ceres
June 25ᵗʰ 1862

We landed at 10 AM yesterday   marched to Grand Gulf 5 miles   there was 4 Regts of Inft two

battery   the Regt in advance fired and killed 5
Rebbels   the Battry fired at six hundred Cavalry
the route was through the woods   part of the way
no road   3 miles from Grand Gulf   the Cavalry
was seen   when the Batry fired three rounds in
quick succession the Batry in the rear and field
Officers went by on the jump   we were wheeled
into Colums cap our guns   supposed we would
have brush   the men were a little startled at
first   it came sudden   a few showed the white
Feather   a chap next to me was sick very sudden
he went into the shade   I took his gun carried it
to G. Gulf   when he over took us he had lost all
his equipment   we arrived at G Gulf 4 PM   our
Boats got there about the same time   there was
no enemy   he had left   our gun boats had
shelled the citty   the inhabitants had all left
we found plenty of live stock   for amusement
the Boys burnt the citty[11]   it is a beautifull sight
two hundred houses on fire at once   we left at
12 PM for Vicksburgh   they expect a tight pull
there   Com Faraguts Fleet is there   Foots Fleet
is above   I had a good meal of fried liver this
morning   shall have some pork fresh for Dinner
I have got 3 hens for supper   I am bad off as
usual   no desire for good things

6 oclock PM   we have come up with the fleet   are
in sight of Vicksburgh

June 26

We have done nothing yet at fighting   I worked with 100 men from 3 til 12 AM   we built a bridge 150 feet long for our Battry to cross on   our Fleet is firing at the citty   the city is full of Battrys   I have not been near enough to see in what position they are

June 27th 9 am

Our boats commenced to Bombard the citty yesturday at 3 P M   continued until 7 P M commensed again this (morning)   the enemy do not return the shot much for some reason or other our men are going to turn the Miss   River by digging a chanel acrost the country ¼ miles long and leave Vicksburgh which is on a hill behind we have got five Hundred Negroes digging now   I will give you a little sketch of our position   now the weather is very warm   been hunting lice all day   found one Body louse big as ox   I am unafraid   I handled him ruff

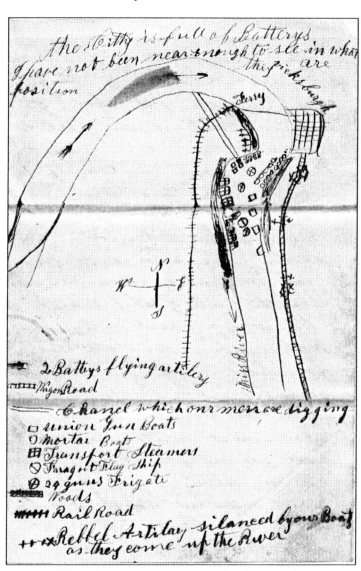

map of battle was drawn on the back of a page
of a letter from Loomis that he received

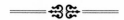

3 PM   the firing is not as lively as it was as   good day   9 Vols   the shells are flying into the city faster than they have done before   I can count 10 shells in the air at once   we are some ways from the mortar boats and the shell   look like stars rising and falling

June 28, 9 AM
At 4 am I got up   found the whole fleet in line in front of the Citty giving them shot   all sorts they are now withdrawing their boats   for what reason I dont know   perhaps if they dont   like the Rebbels guns

6 P M
there has been but little firing since 9 A M   I have been sewing some today and wondering if I wont get a lot of letters from home in a few days

Sun 29
Raining beautifully   we have had no rain of any account but once since we landed on Ship Island the guns are silent on both sides   have been all night   the loss on the Boats has been slight I think   not over ten killed   I dont know what they are waiting for   a mail is going out today and I will bring this letter to a close   I am well and hope you are all the same   will send the rest of my letter at some future time   they intend

to run by the Citty with the mail to night   give
my respects to Ursula and all other that should
take the trouble to inquire   I dare not write any
more   I guess I have writen all the law agrees to
carry for 3 cts   tell mother my mouth has got well
tobacco is very scarce   I paid fifty cts today for
tobacco   a plug that I can buy in Vermont for 5
cts   there is enough but we cant get where it is
write often   I dont mean once a month but once
a week   good by

Yours

Proctor Swallow
Baton Rouge

FIVE
THE BATTLE OF BATON ROUGE AND NEW ORLEANS

The men boarded *The Ceres* and returned to Baton Rouge from the ill-fated mission in July. During the voyage Captain Lorenzo Brooks[12] died. The battered troops hoped to recuperate, but their rest was rudely interrupted by a Confederate force of 5,000 under Gen. John C. Breckinridge who tried to retake the state capital. A morning fog masked the attack on August 5. To defend the town, General Williams had about half his original force of 4000 men. The 250 men of the Seventh Vermont who were still able to fight were posted to the right of the long Union battle line. As Confederate pressure developed on the left, General Williams shifted the Vermonters to help there. They formed a second line of battle behind an Indiana Regiment.

The Vermonters initially feared firing lest they hit the Indiana troops, but obeyed when ordered to do so by General Williams. Major Holbrook described the confused action: "At this time the fog and smoke was so thick that it was next to impossible. Colonel Fullam, who had gone forward to reconnoiter and to ascertain, if possible, the position of the 21st Indiana, was unable to locate it with certainty and could only learn that it had moved further to the right. About the same time some of Manning's guns went into battery in rear of the regiment and opened an indiscriminate fire which greatly endangered our position. Finding the men were so exposed as to be subjected to a heavier fire from our own troops behind than from the enemy in front Colonel Roberts moved the regiment back to its original position in front of the camp."

Colonel Roberts was wounded twice in the action and died two days later. General Williams also received a fatal wound in the battle. Union gunboats on the river finally helped repulse the Confederate attack and a narrow Union victory was achieved. The Seventh returned to Carrollton and renamed the camp in honor of General Williams. The swampy location continued to take a heavy toll on the health of the men and they christened it 'Camp Death'. Major Holbrook was given command of the regiment and promoted to colonel just in time to receive a harsh letter of censure to the unit signed by General Ben Butler himself.[13]

At the height of this tension, another dispute arose with General Butler. Many escaped slaves sought a haven with the Union forces that occupied the area. Gen. Phelps not only welcomed the influx of blacks to the camp, he sought to organize and drill them.[14] When General Butler denied his request for enough muskets to arm three black regiments, Phelps submitted his resignation and departed the military on August 21,

1862.[15]   Shortly thereafter, Gen. Butler reversed his decision and called for raising three regiments of black troops.

While at Baton Rouge the men were able to take furloughs and visit the city of New Orleans. In October, they moved to Camp Kearney a short distance away.[16]

July 30th 1862

Loomis

we returned from Vicksburg the 28   yesturday I got three letters newspapers from you   want I glad   I begun to think you had forgotton me   I also got one letter from a Friend   my health is good thank God   I hope you are all well at home a good many of our men are unwell but I think they are gaining now   our Capt is dead[17]   I am in the Hospital now taking care of the Boys   the weather is warm but pleasant

I got six dollars Pay from the goverment today the first I have had   it wont pay for the tobbacco here   tobacco costs five times as much as it does north   tea is $4.00 per lb   Potatoes $4.00 per bush   every thing else according   I got your stamps   they were very exceptable

I am very buisy   cannot write more than half a letter this time   will do better next time   write often I will write again in a few days   my love

to Mother Fanny[18] and Albion and all others that
inquire   good bye for the presant

From your Friend
P Swallow

Friend Loomis

I will now commence another letter for you   if you
get all that I write you will get sick of reading them
if you can read them at all. I sent you a letter the
last of July land another the 8ᵗʰ of August with
a B. Rouge paper in it   also a NO paper of the 9
by   Col Roberts waitor who was going home to
Rutland   if you get them let me know it

I spent a day looking about the City   had a fine
time   it seemed like being at home at some fair   I
would like to stay in the City longer but it is rather
expencive and you know I must let you a <u>hundred</u>
<u>dollars to build that Barn</u>   cant you wait til I get
my <u>bounty money</u> lemon Ade and ginger Brew is
all that a Soldier can buy here but buy a linen coat
a coton shirt or a straw hat or you are all right to
get anything you call for from a Pickled Elephant
down to a Gin Cocktail

I've got lots of stamps now   going to write often
while they last   the Boys Begged some of me at
first but all at once I lost them all   guess I scolded
you rather hard for not writing but I am sorry
wont do so no more but it was rather Provocing to
have all the boys get some & me none

The Paper I sent you tell you something about the fight we at BR   the Enemy had a larger force than I thought when I wrote before   they had 15 Regts of Inft besides their Artilery and Cavelry against 7 Rgts of us   two thirds sick at that   perhaps they will try to brackfast in B Rouge again

the Prisoners   say they Fair better here than they did in the Confde army   they want to be paroled and not Exchanged   ther was a large crowd on the wharf all the time to look at the Prisoners   we pass a hat around every little while for the benefit of the Prisoners   the People are very liberal   at one time we got over Eighty dollars   don't never get less than fifteen

in speaking of things being high I will tell you what milk 20cts per qt   ½ water   Cheese 50   butter 75 Eggs 75 per doz   Chickens ½ grown   1.50 turkeys 4.00   Ale per lass 20   whiskey 20   lemon ade 10   ice 10 per lb   coton cloth   50   I paid $2.00 for 3 linen hankerchiefs   boots are very cheap now $10 per pair   formaly 25   I was once ofered 15 for mine   hard money is very scarce   when I left BR   I sold my shin plasters for 25cts on the dollar I did not think we would go back   now we are going back   I have the same here   rather Poor speculation guess that wont Build the barn very fast or get the mortgage of the farm

now is the unhealthy part of the year here but it was never known to be any healthyer   I think there has not been a case of yellow fever here this season   quite lucky for us northern chaps   last Sabboth was the first day that seemed like sunday

*in a great while   I could not leave the Boat to go
to church but could hear the Bells   they sounded
like home   I must now close my letter   good bye
for the Present   my best respects to all*

yours

Proctor Swallow

*Midnight   you must excuse me for it is late   I now
put my letter in the box   Proctor Swallow*

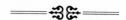

*New Orleans
August 21ˢᵗ 1862*

Dear Sister

*I will write you a few lines as I have plenty of
room but nothing of importance to say   any thing
about the war would only be telling what you must
learn from northern papers a long while before
my letter would reach you   my health is good
and you must be careful of yours   I see by the
papers that the Sec of War has ordered 300,000
men to be Drafted   if true I hope Loomis will
not have to go   I think it is the best thing they
can do to get men enough to whip them and have
it done with   I wonder what the People think
now about marching through the South with only
10,000 men   I suppose that Mrs Wilson could not
well spare Loomis and Barnum   in one of your
letters you spoke of the Dropsy prevailling in your
neighborhood   I hope it will all end well   you*

*know the axideents will happen in the best of
families   tell mother to grow the turkey as large
as she can for I shal come home Hungry as ever
tell Albion I have no fear of his being drafted if
he is as old as he used to be   all persons over
80 are exempt from the military Duty   my best
Respects to Miss Ursula and Uncle Whits folks &
all the rest*

Good bye from your inocent little Brother

*Proctor Swallow
Just see what nice little picture I have sent you of
New Orleans   if you are good girl I may send you
another next time*

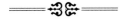

*New Orleans
August 21, 1862*

Loomis

*I take this opportunity to write you a few lines
I am well and wish you all the same   when
I wrote you last I expected to leave here and go
back to Baton Rouge but have not gone yet nor
do I know when we shal   we have nothing to
do but loaf about the city   I have got quite sick
of it   if I could have spent the few days in the
town of Poultney that I have spent here I could
have enjoyed myself much better   I have often
thought it would be a fine thing to be in the City
and have nothing to do but I have traveled until
I am nearly bunderes   besides spent all my*

soap   wonder if I wont have a rich Aunt die
before long   if I stay long I shal want you to send
me a couple of hundred when you sell your wool
I think Buisness is getting a very little liveier that
it was   but it is not very lively yet   things is
not quite as high as they was   I suppose I have
got a mail at Baton Rouge   it left here about the
time we came here   I spent the day at Algiers
yesturday   a small city oppisite N.O.   went into
the Country onto some Plantations   saw some
of the largest mellons I ever saw   water mellons
two fet long and a foot in diamiter   price 50 cts
the cheapest article I find here   there is lots of
Orange and Fig orchards   the trees are loaded
with fruit   Oranges are not yet ripe   Peaches
are plenty at 15 cts each   the weather is very
warm   water poor   we let the River settle and
then put ice in it which makes it very fair   cole
water costs as much here as new milk would in
Vermont   they are unloading a cargo of Ice here
now   it came from Boston I think   I would like
to come and board with you a few days where
I could get plenty of Potatoes   sweet Potatoes
are plenty at a low price but red ones such as
we raise at the north are worth at the market 25
cts per pound   I have got sick of sweet Potatoes
we catch now and then a bull head   they call
them Cat Fish here   I can see no difference but
the size   they weigh from 25 to 125 lbs   it is
fun to catch such Fish as that   musqutoes are
very plenty here   I dont know how much they
weigh but six of them will devour a man in one
night if he is not to large   I bought a few pounds
of maple suggar from the Ship that brought the ice
it tasted like home   but they don' ask anything

*for it   only 50 cts per lb   they are raising Union
troops here now   one Regt is full and one about
half full the 1ˢᵗ 82ⁿᵈ Louisiana Vol   tell me how
Grove is getting along   all the boys that went
from Poultney   there was an Alligator caught
in the River here this morning   the men that
caught him began to skin him   I asked what the
intended to do with it   they told me they were
intending to eat it   I was surprised but beged a
small piece   took it to the Boat cooked and eat
it   if I had not know it was Alligator I should have
called it Fish   I also saw another curiosity in the
shape of a Diving Bell   they are trying to raise
a Revenue Cutter that was sunk when Gen Butler
came up the River   a man went down   staid
about half an hour   a portion of Baton Rouge
has been Burned   Boats are Daily arriving here
with our Commissary stores   if they are atacked
again they will I think Burn the rest of the City and
come down to Carrilton our former encampment
Ships are now arriving here nearly every day
from N York Boston & other Ports   I must tell you
about a little surcomstance that occurred about
the time of the Battle at B Rouge   how a Federal
Col caught some Seseshionist   he put a dress
that resembled a gurilla and went to the House
of some men that he thought might be aiding the
Rebbels and told them that the steamer Burton
(one of our transports) was out in the River & he
wanted them to go out and help to surprise and
capture her   Oh yes they would do any thing to
get a shot at one of them D------D yankees   of
they went   when they went half a mile they
were joined by a Party of Horsemen   supposing
them to be Rebbels they waited for them   what*

was their surprise when they found them to be
Federals but all they could do was to go aboard
the Burton   not captors but as Prisoners of war
the other Prisoners have many a good laugh at
their expence   besides now & then a Bottle of
Whiskey   reports are current that the Rebbels
are evacuating Richmond   also that Ship Island
is taken   both are Probaly without Foundation
the mail closes at 5 o clock to day so I will bid you
good bye for this time   write often   tell me when
you think the war will end   I will write you in a
few days

Yours

Proctor Swallow

it is dog killing time now   the River is full of dead
dogs   it enriches the water very much   when
they get to thick around our Boat we hire a Negro
to tow them to the other side of the River   he
makes $2.00 per day

New Orleans
August 29th 1862

Dear Mother and Sister

In my last letter from Loomis I recd one from each
of you   I have got two letters from mother before

I am very glad to have her write   I hope she will write every opportunity she has

I am glad to hear that you are all well   I hope you will continue so   I am tuff as a Boiled Owl

I don't know as I have any news to write   I understand they are drafting in VT   I think some of the old mugwomps will have to turn out   now good enough for them   they won't find it like staying hehind and spatting on their hands and saying take em Bose

Of course you must give my respects to Ursula and all the rest of the girls for you know I have a large circle of female friends   much obliged for the stamps that I found in your last letter   it will bring this one to you   I hope all them that I had not used that Loomis sent me are bait for fish   but I can get plenty of them at the office here   I sent a letter by James Smith of Hydeville from Ship Island   did you get it   I forgot to tell you that we had a big fire here the other day   the city was on fire at three different places at one time

Good bye

Proctor Swallow

=== ❧ ===

New Orleans
Sept (l862)

Friend Loomis

*Your letter of July 10th was received   would have
got it sooner if I could have seen my company   I
am glad to hear that you are all well   I am well
and have grown so fleshy the past four weeks
the Lieut hardly knew me when he came down
the other day   from him I received your letter   I
sent you a letter the 21st of August   the boat that
took the mail came from NY here in 7 days so I
think you got it by this time if she went back as
quick   I think I have got all the letters you have
sent me up to the 16th of July   I am in better spirits
than I was two months ago when I got no letters
at all   I have had the good luck to loose all my
equipments   gun knapsack and contents blanket
and overcoat   I supposed it with the Hospital
stores   I had been at the Hospital at work before
the Fight of the 5th of August   it was put on board
the Steamer Whiteham¹⁹ which was sunk so by
being a little early and trusting somebody to take
care of thing things they have all gone to the
Devil or to the bottom of the River   it has cost me
$30.00 to get another outfit but then I am getting
$20.00 a month so it won't take long to make that
up   good thing to be getting good wages aint it
the Fedl troops have left Baton Rouge and come
to Carrilton and vicinity 8 miles from here   it is
reported that Stonewall Jackson has got defeated
in a late battle near Richmond   good   I wish*

this Regt might go there and be with the other Vt boys and then I don't think the musquitoes are as plenty as here   things in general can be bought much cheaper than they could a month   business is growing dull   every day many families are fed at the free market   I suppose our Regt has been paid lately   I have not had a chance to sign the Pay Roll so if they have I will have to wait until another pay day if I ever go to camp again I may send you a small order what is due me the first of September

It was forty dollars   I gave the Brigade Quartermaster an order for $30.00 for my things   I got them $4.00 cheaper than I could of our Regt Qt Master   I have got money enough to last me until another pay day but it is not worth a cup if we go ten miles from here   I will send you a sample of it   perhaps it will pass in Vt   the Blue Ticket is the change they use here entirely   now and then you see a dime in silver   I have got twenty dollars treasury Note on the Conf states   I would send it to you but I my have a chance to sell it for five dollars   it is against the order of Gen. Butler to buy or sell it so they have to be pretty careful   Gen Butler and Phelps has had blowup and Phelps has resigned   it was on account of some Niggers that Phelps wanted organize and arm and Butler wanted to have them chop wood and I like his plan the best   let them do the drudgery and somebody else the fighting   I see by the last NY Herald that they copied from a Memphis Paper an account of the Fight at Baton Rouge   they allow that the Ram Arkansas attacked our GunBoat at B.Rouge he 6th of August   and destroyed two and drove the rest *away that Breckenridge also attacked our land forces and captured all the Federal Forces   pretty good want it   The Ram came down the River and then our Gun Boat Essex destroyed it   we also went out on the 6th several miles in search of the enemy   they were not to be found   the prisoners acknowledge tha they had on the 5th a force of 3 to our l and got well whipped at that   it is rumored that Gen Breckenridge is 30 miles above here intending to attack this place N.O.   I don't fancy a shower of bullets any better than any one else but I would like to have him try it on   we have not as many men as he has but we have the advantage of position six miles of Breast Work on our left at Camp Perripet and Lake Ponchatrain on the right I think if he should attack this place it would be his last   I suppose I might as well bring my letter to a close as I don't thin of anything else to wrote write often and write and send all the news*

Yours respectfully

Proctor Swallow

Camp Kearney
October 5th 62

Friend Loomis

I take my pen in hand to write you a few lines I am well   hope you are all well at Home   I have been having the Fever Ague a little lately but guess I have got it cured now   we left Camp Williams Sept 30   we are about four miles from

*there now & about six from New Orleans   Maj
Holbrook is our Col   Capt Peck   Lieut Col   no
maj appointed*

*the news by last steamer is more favorable than
it has been for some time in regard to the war
perhaps I will come Home to plant Corn for you
next spring   the weather is not as warm as it
has been but you cant see much ods (?) yet   I
suppose you have had some good frost in Vt before
now   hope we shall have some here before long
water is very poor when we cant get Ice*

*there is no news to write that I know of   you get
all the war news long before I do   we get Plenty
to eat   can buy most anything that you want
the Camp is lined with Peddlers   yankey Potions
Pies   Cakes   Oysters Fish chicken pies Eggs
Oranges Lemons Apples   Ice cream Ale and in
fact everything you can think of   I can now hear
two or three little brats hollering   Ice Lemonade
we are going to try and have Gov raise our wages
or have the Peddlers lower their Prices   I have
never seen an article here no matter how small
that cost less than five cts*

*when you write again I want you to tell me how
long the war is going to last   it would be mighty
consoling to come home and stay a week   wonder
if they have any Horse trots there this fall   I got a
Wilks Spirit of the times the other day   see that
Eathen was going to trot for ten thousand dollars
which Beat   to day is Sunday   guess wont say
much about horse trotting   our Chaplain that
came with us I havnt seen him for some months*

guess he has gone Home   I dont know that he ever Preached but two or three times   there was one old chap in the Regt that want good for anything   they was going to discharge him but he wouldent go so they made him into a minister   I see the old fellow the other day   he   as though the crows had got a mortegage on him   I guess I will get another sheat   I am going to write lot   cant write again in week   end Vol lst

Volum 2ⁿᵈ Chapter lst

Well I dont know what I am beginning another sheet for as I cant think of anything to write   well Loomis take good care of your self & write three or four times a week and I guess I shall get as much as one of them   Your

from   Proctor Swallow

Chapter 2ⁿᵈ Vol 3ʳᵈ

Well Mother

I will now answer your kind letter which I recieved Sept 4ᵗʰ stating that you had written five times   I have recieved most of them & I think all of them the last I heard from was Sept 7 mailed Aug 25   I am expecting some letters every day now   I want you to be carful of your Health so as to be able to make Pancakes when I get home   I am in hopes we shall have some better times sometime or other we will hope for the best   I have enjoyed better

health than a great many others so I have nothing
grumble at   my two first months was the hardest
but I expect to have somebody conquer between
now and another Spring

well I will close my letter now

Write often
Proctor Swallow

Enclosed find a letter & stamps   have Mr Scribner
direct it to Grove[20]

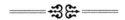

Camp Kearney
Oct 15th 62

Well Loomis

I will not write a few lines to you although it is
but a few days since I mailed a letter   I am well
and hope if I ever hear from you again to hear the
same from you   it is now six weeks since I have
heard from you   there is a mail as often as once
a week   I am getting anxious to hear from you
the weather on the 11th took a sudden turn and
in two hours it was so cold that we had to wear
our Over Coats   it continued cold until to day
I have not slept cold before since we left Stony
Hook last March   there is a report today that
is quite currant that the South has proposed to
compromise with the North   hope they will Hatch
up something to stop the fighting   there is a class
of men that when you talk about Compromise   oh

*no   rather loose every drop of Blood in my vains
they can stretch up their D----D necks and Blow
but let them lay in the Swamps at Vicksburg six
or eight weeks without any tents and not much to
eat except what they stole from the Planters   they
would sing another song   we have lost 30 men in
our Company   one was shot at Baton Rouge   the
Balance by Disease   25 of them have died since
1ˢᵗ of August   the most of them were taken sick
while at Vicksburg   I think that they have done
rong in not sending Discharged Soldiers home
there has been lots of men Died that if they had
sent them home when they ought to they might
have lived   they think about as much of a mans
dying as you would to loose a 3 days calf   they
will cart him out of the way to keep from senting
and thats about all   the chaplain don't often
trouble himself to make a Prear   the Rail Road
runs through our Camp   the train leaves every
half hour for New Orleans   Fare 15 cts   now I
want you to write twice a week until I hear from
you   I dont see why I dont get any letters   there
is a mail about once a week   it is Roll Call   give
my Respects to the Laidies and Albion*

*Good bye
Your Proctor Swallow*
*P.S. Oct 19ᵗʰ have not had a chance to put my
letter in the Office yet   intend to do so tomorrow
just learned that the reason I have not heard from
you in so long   I got a letter from Mr Todd last
night   he says __Baby Boy__[21]   thats good   dont
give him much maple syrup and Pancakes   bring
him up on Salt Punk & hard Crackers so that when
he goes to be a Soldier it wont be so hard for him*

*as it was for me   what are you going to call him
guess better call him Bob or Pat   Mike aint a bad
name   I dont suppose I shall hear from you in an
age   you will feel so big over him   if you call him
any of the names I have mentioned I will give him
my old musket when I get Home   the letter that I
wrote to Mr Todd I recieved an answer in about 20
days   I sent you a letter at the same time   he
tells me he lives alone   gets along well   sold 150
lbs Butter this summer   Butter is worth about 40
cts here now   we get Plenty of Northern Potatoes
now   there is several eating shanties about here
we can get a Plate of mashed potatoes   a cup
of tea 3 Pancakes or warm buiscuit for 25 cts
the Prospect now that we shall leave here soon
Report says Pensacola is our destination but I am
not certain   you may Direct letters to N Orleans
as usual until further Orders   if we move I will
write as soon as we get there   I suppose Mother
is so taken up with the Baby that she could not
read if I should write to her   give my rspects to
Uncle Albion mother Fanny   Granny Swallow &
Baby Loomis   good bye   dont fail to write*

Proctor Swallow

*Enclosed find a letter & stamp   have Mr Scribner
direct it to Grove*

Camp Kearney
Oct 23d 1862

Loomis

*I received your letter of Sept 12ᵗʰ yesterday   was
glad to hear from you and to hear that you was all
doing well   I have writen you two letters within
a week but as I have got one from you I now write
another   this is the first I have heard from you
since the fore Part of Sept but if the Baby dont cry
much I shall expect to hear from you oftener for
the future   the first I heard of the Baby was by
way of Mr. Todd*

*well you spoke about the war ending in your last
letter   you say Slavery must be put down before
the war will end   well it may be so but I have
never heard a Soldier in this Division say that he
was in favor of putting down slavery   there has
been a day when I had some charity for Negroes
but I have none now   if I should live to get out of
this war which I hope I may I should not care to
Enlist again but when they set Slaves free I would
fight to keep them away from the North   the
slaves are here   they are of some benefit here
the only Place in America where they are of any
use I say let them extend it no further but keep
it where it is   if the Slaves were all to be set
free I think the country would be worse of than it
would be to let them be as they are   when I left
home I was of the oppinion as you but the past six
months has altered it some   first the slaves are*

not misused as I had been led to believe   I have seen many that fared better than I have Part of the time this summer   there is not one fourth of them that would work and earn their salt   they are the lazyest   thieveing   lying   stinking set of enss(?) that ever trod the earth   if you had been here as long as I have you wouldent talk of putting down Slavery   I have one thing more to say   that is if the Blacks could be set free and all taken be taken to some Place where they would never get back   say to Africa   I think that would be a good Plan   I dont believe in arming slaves think it will hurt the North more than it would do them good   well we will talk of something else now   you thought I would call you an Abolitionist I guess you would call be a Sesesh   but I am not but I do despise the D...D Niggers   one came to my tent the other day   he wanted to get washing to do   I let hem have a lot   that is the last of him but if I ever do see him   off goes his head

now write often   when I wrote last I did not expect to be here now but I am and may be for some time tell Albion I have got a seseschion watch that he might have but the Express would be two dollars watch is worth 17cts   tell him to come and get it well I must hold up now so give my respects to all

Good bye   you needent put on Phelps Brigade any more

*Yours truly,
Proctor Swallow*

Oct 24th 1862

Dear Mother

I recieved your letter of Sept 5th   was glad to hear from you to hear that you was well   I am well   I had not heard from you in some time you say this war has made you see a great many long Nights   you must try and keep up a good courage as you can   I would rather be at Home than here yet I am not homesick or lonesome   can lay down on my blanket and sleep as contented as I could at Home

you say you would send me some tobacco if you could   I can generally get enough but sometimes it costs very high   if the Soldiers get out of tobacco and money they will get some if it is in the Place where they are   they are bound to have it at any cost   poor old Channsy I feel sorry for him he had not ought to love zyllfy   give my respects to Ursula   should be happy to call on her one of these Pleasant evenings but surcumstances wont admit it now   I am sorry to hear that your old friend Mrs. Ransom is dead

I have got plenty of needles and thread   you needent send any

tell Fanny to be carful of her self and Baby   tell me what his name is

I must bring my letter to a close now   give my respects to all   good bye

Proctor Swallow

Camp Kearney
Oct 30ᵗʰ 1862

Well Loomis

I take my pen in hand this morning to write you a few lines   I am well as usual   hope when I hear from you again to hear the same from you   I recieved a letter from you the other day   the first I had got in a long time   I wrote the next day and sent it by D.C. Barney of Shrewsbury Vt a discharged man in our Co   he is an honest fellow I think you will get it if he gets home   I lent him five dollars which he will Pay to you when he gets ready   the weather is getting cooler than it was   now dont fail to write as often as once a week   you dont know how grattifying it is to get a letter from Home   we are a great ways from home   to see part of the Boys get letters & the rest none makes us lonesome   I will write as often as a mail leaves here   dont let a week pass without writing   I am waiting anciously for a N.Y. Steamer so as to hear from Virginia   one year ago Mclelen was on the Potomac going to exterminate the Rebbel Army   it is about so now what has been done in the year past   well one hundred thousand men have to their last account somebody has taken Norfolk   Ben Butler has taken New Orleans   the whole is not worth one

*mans life   I am in hopes that next May will bring
a change of some kind   I think it must*

Oct 31ˢᵗ

*Well I will try to finish my letter this morning   I
was Homesick yesterday   one of my best friends
had just gone home & I felt very lonesome   but
when I thought of the cold winter in Vt it set me
all right   rather stay here till next May guess
that we can lick them by that time   if I cant come
home at Christmas I like to come by the next 4ᵗʰ
of July   I will close but will write in a few days
again*

*Good bye
Proctor Swallow*

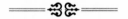

Fanny

*I have heard by the letters from Loomis and
mother that I have got to be Uncle Proc   well take
good care of the little fellow and of your self to for
I intend to come and see you next spring   guess
he will talk some by that time   I want to know his
Name   well good bye   dont fail to have a letter
sent me every week*

Proctor

Dear Mother

*I suppose you have so much baby to attend   that
you dont find much time to write   I am well &
hope to hear the same from you all   I want you
to write as often as you can & I will do the same
keep up good courage for I intend to come Home
next summer   give my respects to Albion   Ursula
and all who may enquire   I must now bring my
letter to a close   no matter if you dont get any
letters from me   keep writing every week*

Proctor

*Camp Kearney
Nov 4ᵗʰ 1862*

Loomis

*I recieved a heavy mail last night   one Envellope
it looks like your writing there was nothing in it
it never was sealed   had one cent stamp on it
if you sent it I would like to know what you sent
in it   have recieved but one letter since Sept 7ᵗʰ
wish you would write every week   I am well
hope you are all well at home   the weather is
comfortable here now   just cool enough   had no
Rain to speak of yet had two Fronts in Oct   give
my respects to all who may enquire*

Good bye for the present

Proctor Swallow

New Orleans
Nov 7th 1862
Since I penned the above I have had no chance
to mail it til now   we have moved to the City   I
think we shall leave here before long   where we
shall go I dont know   I presume Pencacola   the
weather is quite cool   I am well   good day from
your friend

Proctor Swallow

SIX
PENSACOLA, FLORIDA

The Seventh Vermont Regiment was ordered to Pensacola. This port city in the Florida panhandle had been captured by the Union navy in the spring as one of a series of amphibious operations designed to seize key harbors along the coasts of the Atlantic Ocean and the Gulf of Mexico. Part of the Union strategy for winning the war was a naval blockade along the 3549 miles of shoreline between the Potomac and Rio Grande rivers. The Union did not have enough ships to patrol all the harbor and river openings, but the stormy nature of the Atlantic necessitated ports of refuge for the ships at sea. Controlling these critical ports reduced the number of points to be guarded and freed ships for duty elsewhere. It also denied the Confederacy naval yards to build ships for its navy. The army was charged with manning the forts that protected the harbors. Upon arrival, the Seventh began construction of a stockade and other defenses.[22]

Pencacola Fa
Nov 13th 1862

Friend Loomis

Your letter of Nov 10 was recieved a few days since   I was glad to hear that you was well and sorry that you was behind the Snow Storm   your letters are not very lengthy but you are very buisy I suppose   but the evenings are quite long now cant you write a little oftener

I want you to tell me whether you have drawn the money on the Order I sent you or not   the men here say their folks cant get any money on their orders at Home   I want you to tell me if you have drawn enough money to Pay my Debts   if you have who have you paid and how much   I want to know how much you pay each man   I dont know how much I was owing Schribner between 15 & 20 dollars   Wheelock $10.00 and interest Dewey & Dewey $6.00 interest   Scott $15.00 and the Note you Paid ensign

now I think you might time these long evenings to write a little oftener   now think of a poor Devil 40 miles from home and no friends and write often I can write to any body in Poultney twice & get answers from them before I can you once   but never mind

you say you have seen the time that you would have Enlisted but would not now   I think you

are about right on the officers   I think myself
the thing will be settled by Compromise but I am
afraid it will not be done soon enough to suit some
me for one

a report is quite current here that Gen Baxter of
Rutland is in N.O. with power to take this Regt to
Vt   I dont Believe a word of it   yet we have so
many reports we cant believe any of them

I will hold up now   I guess you will have to pay
extra postage

Write often
Proctor Swallow

Pencicola Florida
Nov 20ᵗʰ 62

Well   Loomis

we have arrived here safe & sound a few days
since   it will be our winter quarters I think   it
is said to be a healthy place   I got a letter from
you a few days before we left N.O.   I dont expect
to have a mail very regular here   I have no news
to write   I am well except a little fever or Ague   I
think the men will improve in health here   I wish
we were a little Farther North so that we hear from
seat of war a little oftener   hope it may end soon
I can think of nothing more as I know of   I hope
these few lines will find you all enjoying good
health   take good care of the Baby   my love to
Mother & Fanny Albion and Baby   good bye

Please write often

Proctor Swallow
P.S. I hardly know where to have you direct a letter   I guess to Proctor Swallow   Co I 7th Regt Vt Vol

Pencicola Florid
U.S. Hospital
Pencacola Fa
Dec 5th 62

Friend Loomis

I take my pen in hand this morning to write you a few lines   it is raining nicely   has rained most of the time for the past three days   the first they have had for several months

I am in the Hospital for the first time   some five weeks ago I had dysetery for about two weeks and when I got it checked it left me on my back so weak and poor that I could not stir   I staid with the Co and recieved such care as they could give me for to go the Hospital as it was then would have been worse than my quarters   then we came here   it was a hard jaunt for me   the Surgeon we have had this fall is nothing at all   but thank God since we came here there has two new Surgeons arrived from Vt for this Regt   they are not the men we have had this past Season   <u>take a Pill and go to Drilling</u>   but they look right into a sick mans case and seem to do all in their Power

*for him   if we had had them the Past summer
I think some men who now in their Graves might
have been with us*

*when I wrote to you last I told you I was well   I
was but very weak   I am gaining fast I have been
here   7   yesterday I got down to the Basement
and was weighed   I have gained 8 pounds in
the 7 days   I weigh 109   I must stop writing
now for it is after Noon   I have writen by spels
all day*

*my love to all the Family   will write more next
time   Dr says he will have me well in two weeks
and fat   I feel well now but am weak   do write
often   Direct it to New Orleans*

*good Bye
P. Swallow*

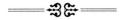

*Pencecola Fa
Dec 9ᵗʰ 1862*

Friend Loomis,

*I take my pen in hand to write you a few lines   I
am in the Hospital yet   But I am gaining fast
shall be out in a few days   a mail has arrived
and there may be a letter in Camp for me   the
mail leaves in a few hours and I dont know as
I have any news to write   it is but a few days
since I wrote a letter but I dont know but you may
get them both at the same time*

the weather is pleasant and just cold enough to be nice   I had ripe straw bury that I picked in the Back yard to day   you cant find that in Vt   the grass is green here as well

guess the war will end in a few days so I will bring my letter to a close

I had a letter from Grove Scribner the other day <u>he says</u> (Proc I will tell you what it is   the fight is all out of me   I have seen enough of it)   well I dont know who has not seen enough

give my respects to all who may enquire

we have got a New Chaplain that came with the Surgeons   he is no such man as the other one was   if a man Dies he will go to the Funeral   I have not time to write any more this time   will do better next time

My love to Mother & Fanny   Bub & the Baby Ursula and all

Good bye
Write often
Proctor Swallow

Pencacola Fa
Dec 12th 62

Dear Mother

*I recieved your letter of Nov 9th a few days since
I had mailed a letter the day before I got this and
there has no mail left since   I am very glad to
hear that you have been well   I have got smart
and am growing fat*

*you speak of Groves having to eat hard Bread
and water   well we have not had much marching
to do but I have lived on hard Bread and water
as much as he has   it was Miss water and the
filthyest stuff   I never saw a beast that drank
such water in Vt   I have eaten hard Bread for
weeks that I had to dig the maggots out of   this
was our living at Vicksburgh with the exception of
what hens and Geee I ccould steal*

*you tell me that Isaac Smith is have a rough time
well he ought to been honest   good enough for
him   I will now close my letter   keep up good
courage   I will come home if I can*

Good bye
Proctor Swallow

======❀======

Pencocola
Nov (Dec) 13th l862

Sister Fanny

I have been writing a little to Mother so I will write
a little to you as I have neglected to write to you
for some time or to Mother   give my rspects to
Ursula   tell Albion that I had to sell his sesesh
watch to pay my taxes   he told Mother to have
me keep it for him but it was gone and the money
spent

I forgot to tell you that the Babys hair came all
nice   it is very beautiful   I admire his Name also
it is better than Bob or Nick

you say Willson & Gazette have got Home   well
they were lucky men thats so   but you say Wilson
cried and you talk as though you thought others
cried to   if you refer to me I can tell you I have not
shed a tear since I enlisted   dont intend to <u>*Bleat*</u>
because I got bit a little   you say you are sorry
for the Poor Soldiers   well farther North they
must have cold toes   but I dont ask any odds of
any body but God

the weather is warm like Oct in Vt   we have had
no Frost since we came here and I have got more
clothing than I could carry if we should moove

you tell me that Mrs. Todd and Hellen have got
home to live   well that is a big thing and bigger

still to think that Mrs. Todd had to come down and sign any such paper as that which she did   well I hope she will go back   and they will live more friendly than they did

well if I live I will try and come Home when the war is ended   so good bye

Proctor Swallow

Pencacola, Fa
Dec 23ʳᵈ 1862

Friend Loomis

Your letter of Nov 26 was recieved the 21   I was very glad to hear that you was all well   but we do not have to dig Potatoes with a crow bar   one morning the Ice on wash Tub was about 1/8 of an inch thick   you say Pit Smith has got Home well he had a good walk   but I guess when I come I shall have a furlow   you say got 5 & l/2 cts for your Hog   you bring your Pork here if you want to sell it   I paid 25 cts for ½ lb of pork   steak I have paid 10 cts per lb   for Porthan Potatoes   Tobacco is worth about three or four times as much as it was North when I left   Butter 75 to cheese 5ct

while I was in the Hospital I had tea or Bread (and rosted potatoes & butter & fresh Fish) if I chose to buy them I could hire my board at home cheaper than I can furnish myself in Butter here   Lieut had to pay $8.00 for a Pair of woolen shirts here but never mind 20 per month & found and a good

*portion   found Dead at that   my old Appatite
which for some time forsook me has returned and
I am getting fat & lazy as usual*

*in one of my late letters I mentioned a report that
Gen Baxter was in N.O.   it proved to be a hoax as
I thought it would   it is reported now that there
been orders forwarded to have this Regt go North
what Place I dont know   if the men dont lie like
the D...L   there is some truth in it but I think we
shall winter here   I rather stay here until warm
weather than to go North   we have cool Nights
some Frosty morning   about such weather as
you get the first part of Oct with very little stormy
weather   I have seen more moon shiny nights
since I came south than I ever saw before*

*you wish I had some of the Liver   I get a piece of
Liver at the market some times & the Regt draws
fresh Beef twice a week or oftener this fall but
I have not been so that I could eat much fresh
meat for the past three months   I have eaten
considerable fresh Fish since we came the only
meat the Doctor allowed me to eat   I could live
on fresh Fish   I have got a Bully Appatite now
could eat a Nigger Funeral corpse and all*

*I have been getting more letters from you lately
than common   well keep writing   I write as
often as the mail goes   I want you to eat some
of that good syrup for me   when I went to NO
last Aug if had supposed me were going to stay
as long as we did I should have sent for a box of
syrup and sugar   straw bury sauce and tobacco
there was a good many Boxes come to N.O. this*

fall for the men from Home   but I shall not try to get any thing until I think we are going to stay somewhere about two months

it is getting near Pay Day   the men have not been Paid in four months   I shall get 8 months Pay $24.00   the place here is rather dull   it may be as large as East Rutland   about as much buisiness done as in East Poultney   the 6th Regt N.Y. Vols known as Billy Wilson Zouaves the hardest set of men that ever left NY City   so hard that when the Regt got Ready to leave   Wilson addressed the Regt & told them if there was a man that considered himself Honest to leave the ranks   were here when we arrived but left when we came here   they raised hob all the time   they went to N.O. where it took two or three Regts to keep them quiet   two or three got shot and as many hung   and about 50 went to Fort Jackson

goodbye for this time
Proctor Swallow
I was intending to send Mother & Fanny a sheet but I not got time as my letter must go right of now or not at all...respects to Ursula   Albion and the Baby   good bye

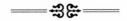

Pencacola Fa
Dec 30ᵗʰ   1862

Dear Sister Fanny

You kind of Nov 20ᵗʰ was recieved a few days since   I had intended to answer it when I wrote to Loomis but I did not begin in time as the mail closed one day sooner than I thought it would what did you get in your stocking Christmas   I got _and it was well sweetened   for supper me had an Oyster stew and some lemon Pie   I might as well wish you Ursula Bub and Baby a happy New Year   Christmas is past so I wish you Mary Fuller   would wish you as warm & pleasant weather as we are having of it would do you any good but it would not   it is just like summer

we are quartered in large nice House 50 rods from the   Village on a rise of ground   it is quite Pleasant   two Cos are quartered here   the Bal of Regt in other Buildings   there is 10 in the room I am in   we have a nice Fire Place but dont need much fire

you spoke about our Regt coming North   I cannot tell what we shall do   I would like to stay here till warm weather & then go North

I would like to have you if you can get any of my money more than to Pay my debts get some woolen Cloth as near the color as you can of a Piece I will send you and make me a Pair of Shirts & a Pair of

Drawers   I want good Coth and near the color of that I send   you can tell something about the size by Loomis   I am about his size   guess I want the Shirts fair length and good size so that when you wash them they will not be to small   I want them for the outside not for under shirts   the collar as much as 2 ½ inches wide   ristbands about the same width   4 buttons on Boosom   one on collar make collar such shape as I sided to have it made cut out in front   Drawers band around the top with four buttons   legs to large at bottom   split them at Bottom   put some tape on for strings   I want 2 good pair woolen socks   split the Drawers behind 3 or 4 inches on back and put in some strings   I have told you how I want then as near as I can   you must use your own jugment and if you think I am wrong make it right   a good Pair of woolen Shirts cost $8.00 here when you get them made   keep them til I write for them   which will be when I get somewhere   where I know we will stay a few days   I may not want them in two months   if you can make them tell me in you next letter   the Shirts they give us now are Poor white things   2/3 cotton   Ive got 2 shirts   they will last me some little time yet

Good bye
Proctor Swallow

Write often   direct to N.O. as usual

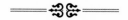

Pencacola Fla
Jan 20th 1863

Friend Loomis

*I take my pen in hand to write you a few lines   I
recieved a letter from Fanny & Mother last night
but did not see any of your writing in it   I was
glad to hear that you was all well   I am well also
the health of the Regt is better than it has been in
a long time   why dont you sit down some evening
and write if you cant find time to write days   I
dont get much war news so I want you to tell me
about the war   I know you can find time to write
when the evenings are as long as they are now*

*we had a snow storm here the 16th   it snowed
quite briskly for half an hour   they have had no
snow but three or four times in 15 years*

*I had another letter from Grove Scribner last night
he is well but has got sick of the war   the report
has been that we were coming North but I think
not at Present   I think we may go in the Spring
tell Mother to send me some Gould Thread and tell
me how to use it for a sore mouth   I must bring
my letter to a close   I will write more in a few
days   give my respects to all the folks   good
bye*

Yours from
P.Swallow

Pencacola Fla
Jan 30ᵗʰ 1863

Friend Loomis

*I take my pen in hand this morning to write you a
few lines   should writen before if there had been
any Mail   I am in hopes there will be a mail Boat
in soon as I should like to hear from you and from
the Army in Va   I have heard but little about
the war since Gen Burnside took Command of the
Union Forces   I think that 7ᵗʰ Vt may possibly go
North this Spring   I hope that it may*

*they had a Greased Pig with a Prize of $5.00   also
a slipry Pole with a prize of $10.00 and a foot race
the prizes were all won by diferent individuals in
the Regt   I think is good thing to give the men
a chance to try their speed and limber up their
joints*

Feb 1ˢᵗ 63

*I will now finish my letter   a mail has just arrived
but I got no letters   I think I have recieved two
letters since I came here from you   it is 3 oclock
just one year ago I parted with you at the Depot
as we left Poultney for our Camp in Rutland   I
think health of the Regt is better than when we
came here   we have only half the Men that we left
home with March 10ᵗʰ 62   my health is getting
very good   I have done no Duty yet   have been
troubled with the Rheumatis in my Hips   my
health other ways is very good   the Officers are*

*very kind to me   I always tried to please them
and never tried to shirk from Duty when   well
they have never allowed me to do anything since
I first began to have the Fever Ague last Oct   I
find there is another class that do not fare as well
as I have*

*Fanny wished to know if I knew Hobart Hosfords
boy   I did not know him   I had a letter today
that got overlooked yesterday   it was dated Jan
7th   was glad to hear that you was well   the mail
is going to leave in a short time   so I will have to
close   give my respects to the family   good bye*

*Yours
Proctor Swallow*

SEVEN
SANTA ROSA ISLAND

Santa Rosa was an alligator-infested island in Pensacola Bay. It was felt that it would take a smaller force to guard the harbor and navy yard across the bay in Pensacola from there. Fort Pickens on the island was one of the two important Federal installations in the South to remain in Union hands throughout the war. It was the headquarters of the West Gulf Blockading Squadron, a vital station for repairing and coaling vessels, and a depot for naval stores. In February the Seventh Vermont Regiment set up camp just outside the fort on the westerly side of the island.[23]

Fort Pickens
Santa Rosia Island
Feb 22nd 63

Friend Loomis

I take my pen in hand to write you a few lines your letter of Jan 16th has come to hand   was glad to hear that you was all well   my Remmatis are better   we left Pencacola the 19th and came here we are on an Island 7 miles from Pensacola   it is 60 long and sandy like Ship Island   you must not worry if you do not hear from me reggular as the mail is not to be depended on   I will write as often as I can   you must do the same

they are firing a salute from the Fort in rememberance of Washington birth

I should like to come home and help you make suggar this spring but shant be able as business of importance detains me here   sort of an engagement with Uncle Sam   yet I may be with you when you least expect it

I have given up all hope of the Regt going to Vt until discharged   it may go to Ftress Monroe and it may not   I do not get as much News from the war as I should like to but it seems to be drawing to a close very slow   I always placed my confidance in McClelen but I learn that he has been dismissed from the army in disgrace as well as some others and I think there is plenty more that deserve the same and worse fate   I dont think we are any nearer Richmond than we <u>was</u> one year ago   besides I think the Rebbels are in better condidion than they was a year ago   I should like to have it desided by one day Fighting take the whole army and kill or get killed and have that end it   you see it dont hurt a man much to be killed with a 13 inch bom shell   I saw a man hit with a six lb ball only and he never asked who threw it   strange want it that he did not say anything about it

*well I will bring my letter to a close   give this to
mother and all the indoor folks   tell Albion if he
wants to know what fun is he had better Enlist
right off for $20.00 a month & no lost time   have
not done a days Duty in five months   get just as
much Pay as them that work   yet good health
& less Pay would suit me better   good bye write
often*

from your friend
P.Swallow

*P.S. direct to Proctor Swallow
Co I 7ʰ Regt Vt Vols
Fort Pickens
Santa Rosia Island
Florida*

*Ft Pickens Fa
Apr 1ˢᵗ 63*

Friend Loomis

*I take my men in hand to write you a few lines
I am well   hope this will find you all enjoying
good health at Home   I have not been so well as
I am now in six months   I have just begun to do
Duty   the first I have done in five months   I left
Pencacola ten days since   they have Evacuated
the Place   most of the Inhabitants have left the
Place and come over here to the Navy Yard for
protection   a part of the City was burned before
I left and I attended the fire and got me a good
Matress and Pillow so I am in town as far as a bed
is conserned*

the Barrels that was sent from Poultney have arrived   they had been Broken open and a good share of the things stolen   Capt Clark lost all his clothes   my shirts and things have gone to the D...l   I did not get the first thing out of either Package   the Regt has not been Paid since Sept 1*st* 62 and the Prospect is fair not to be for some time to come   the last letter I got was dated Jan 31   I must close   the mail closes at 5 O clock and I shall have to hurry to get my letter to the Ft in season so with my Respects for the family I will bid you good day   write often

Proctor Swallow

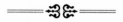

Fort Pickens
*Apr 3*rd* 63*

Friend Loomis

I take my pen in hand to write you a few lines   I mailed a letter 3 days since but I understand there is a mail going to leave here at 11 O clock today so I will write you a few lines more   recieved a letter from you today   you wanted to know how the Plumleys was getting along   they are both tuff as Boiled Owls   you also spoke of a Griswold in the Regt   I know nothing about him   old Heap has gone under the sod   he Died at Pencacola you ask if I am out of the Hospital   I am and am doing Duty   the first I have done in about six months   I am not as strong as I was but other ways I am as well as ever *you Farmers are getting rich   I guess $1.00 per lb for wool $10.00 for sheep   no taxes to pay*

tell Fanny I rec some Gould Thread in my last letter   she said she had sent me some once before but I did not get it yet

I would like to have you send me ten dollars if you can   we have had no money for a long time & dont know as we shall ever be paid again   send in U.S. Treasury money and if we ever get Paid so there will be any money in the Treasury I will send you some Orders   put it in a letter direct to me Co I 7ᵗʰ Regt Vt Vols Ft Pickens Florida care of Capt Clark and I will run the risk of getting it   you ask if we got the Rebbels whipped   not yet   we have not been troubled with Rebbels since we came to Pencacola   I understand they are quarrelling near Vicksburgh but dont know much about it   I must close now   give my love to the Family   good bye

Proctor Swallow

*Santa Rosa Island Fla
May 13ᵗʰ 63*

Friend Loomis

I take my pen in hand to write you a few lines I cannot write much as I have but a short piece of Paper your letter of Apr 13ᵗʰ has come to hand was glad to hear that you are as well as you are but a bad cold is bad enough   I am enjoying very good health at Present but Oh Dear how the cursed Fleas do bite   but we have one consolation it feels good to scratch   I write a line and then scratch then write another   Oh Gosh one is biting like thunder now   well I have broke his Back and will try to finish my sheat

a Darkey was comeing from the Hospital the other day on Horse back and did not choose to halt at the Command of the Picket Guard and was Shot through the arm   he concluded to stop   the Adgt tried to pass the Picket one Night and was fired at but not hit   our Hospital is l ½ miles from Camp and beyond the Picket Guard

there is strong talk of Consolidating the 7th Vermont into five Companys   the Officers & non commissioned rendered supernumary will be Discharged from the Service   they will keep the smartest so I dont stand much chance to get home do you think

our chaplain is taking a great deal of pains with the Men   he tries to make Christians of the Men BUT we have writing Schools spelling Schools Licams (?) and Prear meetings nearly every Night it is a good thing for one half of the men that can write their Name

I am getting to be quite a Tailor   have cut and made several Pair of Pants and two Vests   I am going to make you a Vest and send to you as soon as I get time   it is getting prety warm here and I have got a lot of white Pants to make   white

Linen is two dollars per yard   they are very cool and nice

I have never took of my woolen shirts or Drawers & dont dare to now for fear of Rheumatis

I would like to know if you heard from Uncle L. B. Swallow if so where is he and how did he get along with the affairs that you wrote to me about

You said that you heard that Dan Ensign had Enlisted   is it so   does Mr Scribner live on the old Place and how is he getting along   how does Mrs Todd folks get along

we got Paid off a short time since   got lots of Soap now   dont you wish you was a Soldier   I was owing considerable but not so much as some of the Boys   I lent a man five dollars for which I get ten Pay Day   some of the men were owing more than they had due them   there is two months Pay due me now and I have got fifty dollars in money I dont intend to be as hard up for money for three months to come as I have for three months Past I have got nearly as fat and lazy as when I left Home   had pretty easy time this summer   have done no Camp duty   have to do but sew and no more of that than I choose to do

Is there any prospect of the war comeing to a close up your way   if so let me know

good bye
Proctor Swallow

Camp Stoughton Fla
May 23ʳᵈ (1863)

Friend Loomis

I take this opportunity to write you a few lines   I
am well   I hope these few lines will find you all
well at Home   I have had no letters from you in
some time   I expect one soon   I suppose you
are getting your Corn in the Ground now   well I
have got no Corn to Plant but am very buisy most
of the time hunting Fleas   you have no idea how
they do torment us   if you could hear the oaths
that are uttered on account of this little insects you
would think the men were poor Christians   get
up any time of Night and you will find some one
out shaking their Blankets   in sifting one bushel
of sand I do believe you would get five pecks of
Fleas   you can kill one half a dozen times and
then he wont be dead   perhaps you may think
this is a Fish story but they are as hard to kill as
that cat that I have heard tell about

they took her to the stone wall and pounded her
head until she was dead and left her   the next
morning she was at the door all right   they killed
her several times but it done no good so they cut
her head off and was their surprise next morning
to find her at the door with her head in her mouth
mew mew   but enough of that

we are having much finer times than we did last
year   I have no desire to come North at present   I

*might have come Home last Spring if I had wished
to but am glad I did not   my health was never
better*

June 5ᵗʰ 63

*I commensed a letter a few days but did not mail
it as there was no chance so I will finish it now
a mail leaves to Day for N.O.   I dont know as you
will get this as I have not heard from you in so
long that I suppose you have gone to some Forign
Country or all dead   is any of the Swallow
family alive   if so I should like to have you tell
me how they are getting along*

*I hear that Gen Hooker has had some sharp
fighting in Va   dont know the result but hope he
has Killed some body   it is reported that Stonewall
Jackson is dead   if so the Confederates loose a
brave man   I must lose   if you get this write as
I should like to hear from you   direct as usual
I am still in the 7ᵗʰ Vt   good Day*

Proctor Swallow

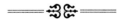

*Camp Stoughton
June 5ᵗʰ 63*

Loomis

*I have received a letter from Fanny and Mother   it
contained a few lines from you   also ten Dollars
in money   am much oblige to you for your trouble
enclosed you will find an Order for Nineteen
Dollars on acct of Henry Beebe   Present it as*

soon as you get it and if you cannot get the money
on it let me know immediately and send the order
back   if you get the money I want you to send
me a good silver hunter Watch as you can get for
$15.00 fifteen dollars of American manafacture
my Watch was stolen from me when I was bathing
put it into a little box and send it by mail   I think
an ambrotype case would be a good thing to send
it in   do it up in good shape   I want a lever
watch   if you have no buisiness at Rutland go to
Chafees and charge your expense to me

P. S

EIGHT
FORT BARRANCAS

Fort Barrancas on the mainland across the bay from Santa Rosa Island was the next destination for the men of the Seventh Vermont Regiment. Company I rotated service on a redoubt that protected the entrance to the bay with its large guns. The men were on picket duty every other day and worked on the fortifications. In addition they practiced infantry and artillery drills. During this period there was much discussion as to the actual date their enlistment began. Was it when a man enlisted or when he was mustered in? The issue was resolved by the State Legislature which decided the expiration date was June 1, 1864. The pros and cons of re-enlisting were also widely debated. The soldiers were offered a bounty, a furlough in Vermont, and the right to call themselves a Volunteer Veterans Regiment if they would re-enlist. In the end thirty-five, all but fifty-nine of the surviving original members of the Seventh Regiment, re-enlisted.

On September 10th, I Company experienced a serious accident while servicing an eight-inch seacoast howitzer gun at the redoubt. It exploded prematurely killing one man and seriously injuring another.[24]   Also, at this time, the troops at Barrancas were quarantined to protect them from the yellow fever epidemic racing through the navy yard. Communication with the outside world was cut off as no vessels were allowed to enter the port, thus mail and supplies were not received.[25]

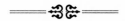

> *Ft Barancas Redoubt Fla*
> *June 25th 63*

Loomis

I recieved your letter of May 25th last Night   also one from Grove Scribner   my health is good this summer   I am doing Duty   we left the Island a few days sinc   came here   we are in a redoubt Fort 1/2 mile from Ft Barancas acrost the Bay opposite Fort Pickens   the Regt is in Camp near here

Co I & C are in the Redoubt   Co A & D at Ft Pickins

you mentioned the money you sent   I got it all right   sent you an order for $19.00 on acct of Henry Beebe for Alloted Pay   if you get it I wish you would send me the Watch as soon as you can for it is handy to have a time piece on guard

give my respects to all who may enquire   I can write but little for I am on Guard to Day   will write more next time   good bye

Proctor Swallow
Please send me 4 yds of Velvet Ribbon as wide as the Piece Enclosed

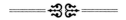

Barancas Redoubt Fla
July 5th 1863

Loomis

I take my pen in hand to write you a few lines   I am well and hope these few lines will find you all well at Home   I recd a letter from Home last evening reporting the folks all well except Loomis had a lame Back   Fanny mentioned half a Doz men that was going to help you Shear Sheep guess you have been enlarging your flock

yesterday was the 2nd fourth of July that I have spent in the employ of Uncle Samuel   hope I shall live to spend a good many more

Gen Lee I suppose is in Penn   I think it will be a good thing for the People at the North will get their Eyes open about the time he gets to NY   I hope he will go there and stir up them Copperheads

I think I have got the start of you this year   I had new Potatoes Cabbage and string Beans five weeks ago   Peaches Mellons Cowcumbers and Tomatoes are ripe   all they ask for Cowcumbers and peaches is 10 cts each   Cabbage 50 cts per Head   Potatoes $1.00 per peck   Whiskey 2.00 a smell   you can get a Watermellon as big as a

Hogshead for 25 cts   Mellon vines do well in this Land where it is so poor that weds wont grow

I suppose you are beginning to cut your grass   I can sit in the cool shade as I have no grass to cut Blessed be nothing   dont you wish you was a Soldier   I must close now   give my respects to all

Good Bye
Proctor Swallow
P.S.   direct to Fort Barancas Florida

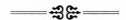

Fort Barancas Fla
July 16th 1863

Friend Loomis

I take this oppertunity to write you a few lines   I am well yes Healther than I have been since I left Vt   I am living pretty easy   have no Co Duty to do   can sew as much or as little as I please   I have been on Guard but three times since last Oct I am looking for my Watch every day

Vicksburgh Surrendered on the 4th of July with 27,000 Prisoners and a large amount of Guns Port Hudson has since fallen but you no doubt heard of it before I did   I presume Mobile will be their next jump   if they sucseed in taking it they will them pretty well cleaned out in these parts   we have numerous reports in regard to Gens Hooker & Lee   one day Hooker is whiped

*the next it is something else   the last report was
the Rebbels had concluded to take Washington if
they could*

*the Health of the Regt is good this summer   we
have lost no men in Co I since last Jan*

*I suppose you are walking into the Hay all sorts
about now   I wish you had your dairy down here
could sell your milk for 25 cts per qt   gosh how
Rich you could get   guess you had better drive
them   down here and try it awhile   you would
get Rich nearly as fast as we Soldiers do*

*how does Widdow F & Dan Culver get along   I
fear there will be a surplis of women when the war
is over   perhaps it will be a good thing for some
such fellows as me that could not get married
when there was any boddy else around   dont
you think so*

*guess I wont stop to write any more till you see
if you can read this   give love to all the Family
should like to have you send me an ambrotype of
that youngster of yours*

write soon   good Night

> *From
> Proctor Swallow
> Co. I 7Vt Vols
> Fort Barrancas
> Florida*

Barrancas Florida
Aug 16ᵗʰ 1863

Loomis

I take my pen in hand to write you a few lines   I
am well   hope these few lines will find you all
well at Home   I have not heard from you since
the last time which was some little time ago   I
have seen a list of several of the towns that have
stood a draft but not of Poultney   I saw a list of
Fairhaven   in it was Fayette & Chauncey Wood &
Josh Hard   would like to know if you are Drafted
we are going to have our Regt filled   the Col is
going to Vt in a few days to get the men[26] *I have*
hard that Charles Ramm is Drafted   hope he
will have to come a print   the men are expecting
to have some fun with Conscrips but I guess they
wont find them so green as they think   for my
Respects to all who may enquire

Good Bye
Proctor Swallow

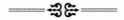

Barrancas Fla
Sept 5ᵗʰ 1863

Loomis

I recieved your letter of Aug 10 this hour and
hasten to answer it   I am well   you may not
have another letter in some time for the Yellow

Fever has got around and ther is little or no communication with other Ports   they have had some cases at the Navy Yard one mile from here no sitizens are alowed inside our lines and we are not alowed to go outside   it is so late in the Season   I do not think it rage much   hope it will not get into our Regt

I got the List of drafted men you sent me but had seen one several weeks ago   I got a letter from Grove Scribner to Day   he sent me a list of the same men   he is well   I think there will be a chance to send this letter today but dont know good by   respects to all

Proctor Swallow

Redoubt Barrancas Fla
Sept 13th 1863

Loomis

I take my pen in hand to write you a few   I am enjoying the best of health   the Yellow Fever has pretty much Died away   none of the Soldiers had it   we had a sad axident in our Company a few days ago   while firing an eight inch Colombian at a target the vent was not properly thumed   it went off   James B. Royce had his left arm off and badly burned in his face   lef side   recovery doubtful Robert Ripley loses his Right hand   they were from Shrewsbury Vt   the men are no as careful as they should be   if the men are at ther proper place they cannot more than loose a hand or fore arm the weather is pleasant and warm enough for comfort but little Rain of late   there is no news of importance   we are looking for the Pay master this is six months Pay Due us now

give my respects to the folks   write soon

Good bye
Proctor Swallow

Sept 20th 1863

Friend Loomis

I take this opportunity to write you a few lines I am not dead yet   the Yellow Fever has gone away from us   there is no news of importance we have had not mail in a long time   expect one soon   one of the men that was hurt firing the Gun died   he is buried to Day   his arm was broken near the Shoulder badly but it was not taken off quick enough and it mortyfied   the one that was hurt the worst will get well I think   I wish the folks would get me up a Pair of Wolen gloves   not a very heavy Pair   send them by mail   I would like them to wear this Winter

Well guess that is all   give my respects to all

Good bye
PoctorSwallow

═══ ❧❧ ═══

BarRancas Fla
Sept 29th 1863

Loomis

I take this oppertunity to write you a few lines I am well   have not heard from you in some time   we have been Paid off   I have sent you per Express $150   one Hundred and fifty Dollars use it as you like   write me as soon as you get it   dont wait til next week   if you have sent me that Watch well and good   if not   dont mind about it   when I want any thing and intend to get it the same year   perhaps I will send to you for it   if I had it now it would be worth Ten dollars more to me than it will now   I waited some time and bought me one and if that had come before we were Paid off I could sold it   well the last time you wrote me you said you was going to send it next week   if you had not waited it would have been here long ago   if Mother wants any of that money let her have what wants   my Respects to all

Proctor Swallow

—❧ ❧—

Barrancas Fla
Nov 2nd 1863

Friend Loomis

*I received your letter of Oct 11th   also the Watch
I am well pleased with it   I wound it up and it
went to talking right off   also the Velvet that
Fanny sent me   I guess I scolded some in my
last letter but you must consider who it come from
besides I will take it all back and beg* <u>*Pardon*</u>

*I sent you some money $150   the first of Oct
write as soon as you get it   my health is good
so is that of the Regt*

*Fanny wrote me that Hall of this Company has
been in Poultney and that she might have sent me
some things if she had seen him   well I am glad
she did not see him*

*when I sent you my money I supposed I had kept
enough for myself but I find that I am short now
if you get my money and it is convenient I wish you
would send me Twenty dollars in Green Backs   I
want you to send it right off or not at all for I do not
like to be waiting for any thing to long   send it by
mail and I will run all Risk   my Respects to all*

Good Bye
Proctor Swallow

Barrancas Fla
Nov 3ʳᵈ 1863

Loomis

I wrote you a letter yesturday telling you that I had received your watch & velvet that you sent me but I did not write all that I meant to   I have concluded to try and get a Box from Home   now I want some things and I cant get them here   so I will have you send them to me   it does not matter what the things cost   I want them sent in good shape

I want a can that will hold 5 or 6 lbs of Butter and Part of a good Cheese   some Maple Suggar or some Maple Molasses   1 Pint of Perrygorric some Camphor Gum   two dollars worth of Opium one pound of salts   <u>two qts of the best Brandy</u> you can get and 5 or six Doz of Eggs   put the Eggs into a small Box by themselves   put the small Box into the Big one   I guess you had better Pack them in fine salt   the small end down   I want a can of Honey and if you have got any sausage meat   Put me up a can of that   would like a few cans of Preserves (Levi Plumley has just come around where I am writing and says tell Loomis I am alive and kicking)   and some Dried Berries (no Dried Apples)   dont care if you send me a green one or two for I have not seen one since last winter

3 or 4 Handkerchiefs and towel   12 Hanks of Black linen thread   6 sticks Black silk twist for button holes 6 scanes Black sewing silk not very fine   6 Hanks white linen thread   l0 yds of the same kind of velvet that you sent me last and a yard and a half of cotton Velvet cloth   I want you to be shure and get a yd and a half so that I can get strips 50 inches long

I want a pair of cotton shirts with linen Boosoms no collar and 4 wide turn over collars   Fanny will know about what size to get them   I bought a pair of Wollen shirts the other day for only $9.00 <u>dirt cheap</u>   have the stuff that you send in cans all soldered up snug   send good lot of cases Put the things in a good strong Box   put some Hoop Iron around the ends   put it in the Express Office and Pay the express on it   I rather Pay twice as much to have the things Put up in good shape and get them than half Price and loose them   send it right away and be shure and send the cost and I will send you the money the first time we get Paid off which I think will be soon as I shall get the Box   mark it Plain

Proctor Swallow
Fort Barrancas,Florida
Co I 7th Regt Vt Vols

Mark it on two sides   I wish you would asertain when the 7th Vt Regs time of service expires   some say June 1st 1864   others Feb 12th 1865   I am no particular about staying a few months in the Army but would like to know how long we have got to stay

Send four Doz Pants   Buckles   cheap kind

send me six Pair good suspenders

let me know what the things cost

Fort Barrancas
Nov 29ᵗʰ 1863

Friend Loomis

Your letter of Nov 5ᵗʰ has come to hand   I received it the 24ᵗʰ only 15 Days getting through   you had but little to say and that was to the effect that you wished me to come Home and work the Farm while you served your time as a Drafted man   well if you get drafted in Jan next I cant do it for I do not think my time expires until Feb 12ᵗʰ l865   guess you must buy a Substitute   you know that money will do most anything and I suppose you have got lots of it by this time as they tell me that Cheese is selling for 12 cts and Butter 25 and Potatoes 50 wool 65   so I think you must have more money than you can take care of some of the men are feeling rather down in the mouth they supposed until lately that their time was out in June next   they dont like it at all   Mother said that Mr. Scribner wanted to know if Austin Taft was in the Regt   I guess she meant Lewis Taft he is in Co D   we have had a light Frost once this fall   the sun is shining bright and warm   just right for comfort   I wish you would send me a box of Herricks suggar coated pills   send them in a letter   if it will not hold them all at once send them at twice   well I guess that is all for this time   give my respects to all that may enquire write soon

Good Bye
Proctor Swallow

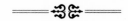

Fort Barrancas
Dec 11 1863

Dear Mother

I now take my pen in hand to write you a few lines to let you know that I am yet among the living and enjoying as good health as usual and hope the Lord has been no less mercyful to you   in all my letters from Home I find a welcome sheet from you I hope you may be able to continue them for a long time to come   there has been speculation among the Boys here as well as the People at Home in regard to the time we should again see Vermont at 4th of July they think the next Christmas and when Christmas is past they talk of July again and so it goes   yet here we are and are likely to stay here or about here for some time to come but that is not so bad as might be for most of the men are enjoying good health which is one of the greatest Blessings that God can bestow upon man once I did not know how to prize good health but I trust I have not lived the past two years without learning something *you ask me how I am living   if I get enough to eat   we in Co I and Co C are quartered here in the Redoubt   we have good casemates to stay in have got a stove in the one I am in and Windows in the Port Holes   there is six of us stay here and we are as comfortable as we should be in a good Brick House at Home   as far as eatables we are living well considering we are in the Army   we get Potatoes once a Day   fresh Beef twice a week Onions twice a week   fresh Bread every Day and any quantity of Tea Coffee salt Pork & Beef or <u>mule meat</u> as some of the men choose to call it   we can buy Condensed milk for 50cts per can of about half a pint   a tea spoonfull is enough for a pint of Coffee   we get Butter for 50 cts per lb   Cheese for 40   fresh Fish is plenty   Oysters 50 cts per 100 in shell   we can get Flour at the Bakery for 6 cts per lb   we have Pancakes & Doughnuts as many as we choose to buy materials to make them Charles Murling of Poultney does our Cooking for the co now with the help of a Black African*

he is a very good cook   we have a large stove with an oven   can have baked Beef & Beans & you know I never was very fond of good Roast Beef & SpareRib   Eggs are 1.00 to 1.25 per Doz cant often get any at that

I wrote to Loomis some time ago for a Box of things shall look for it about New Years   there is some talk of letting the men of this Regt or those that choose to Enlist into the Veteran Corps   thus they will get 402 Dollars Bounty and not have to serve only two years longer than they would in this Regt but I have not concluded to Enlist yet   I prefer to get out of this before I get into any thing else besides I am not the tuff and rugged Chap that I once was and should make a poor show if I had to go through with my first six months Soldiering again   but thanks to a good Captain I have not done any Guard Duty or Drilling since a year ago last Oct unless I did it for my own Pleasure which was not often   <u>I recon</u> I am reported on Daily Duty and do Sewing for the Boys   I dont have to do it for nothing mind you   labor is not as cheap as it used to be North   for making a Pair of common Pants without lining I get 1.50   1.40 to

2.00 for making a Vest and other things accordingly I cannot cut a Coat of Vest but I can cut a Pair of Pants by Rule which is more I guess than any other Swallow can do   there is a Regular Tailor at the fort and I learned to cut pants of him   I have work enough to keep me buisy most of the time   so I live prety easy and get money enough to buy a good many things that I should otherwise have to do without or use my Gov Pay   now I think I have given you a fair statement in answer to your enquiries of how I am getting along   as for clothing we get enough from the Gov such as it is and other things we can buy

well I have just eat supper and will finish my letter had some biscuit for supper and some stewed Berries that Jimmy Oakman had sent from Home we have got six large Redfish   enough for the Company a Dinner tomorrow   we are going to have them stuffed and baked   and tomorrow is Butchering Day and I am going to have some fried Liver for supper   can get a whole Beef Pluck for

50 cts   you know I did not used to eat any fried Liver at Home but I can eat a very little now   the next Day is Sunday and dont know what I shall do that day   it is to far ahead to go to Church   I presume the Regt had got log Houses to stay in this winter   six in all   two Companies are at Ft Pickens 2 miles from here

there was a Cavelry man got his Back up the other Day and shot himself with his Revolver   the charge went clean through his right Breast out through the Back   yet the Poor Devil is getting well now

Perhaps you would like to know when to look for me home   if I should live until a year from Next Feb I think I shall get Home   dont expect to before unless the war closes and I have no idea that it will   I must now bring my letter to a close as I am in something of a hurry   you must excuse me for writing so short a letter   when I get time I will write some more   give my Respects to your Children and Grand Children and all others who may enquire   so with my best wishes for you all I say good Night   write soon

Proctor Swallow

=== ❧❧ ===

Fort Barrancas Fla
Dec 16th 1863

Friend Loomis

*I take my pen in hand to write you   I am well
hope you are all well at Home   we got a mail day
before yesturday and one yesturday   I was lucky
enough not to get any letter   I learn from those
that had letters from Home that they are holding
out large inducements for men to Enlist   dont like
the idea of Drafting*

*I guess they say that the Towns are Paying four
and five hundred Dollars to Vols besides the
Government Bounty taxes must be very low   I
think well that is the way to do it   I hope that there
will be no Draft   If this Regt could be discharged
now every man would Enlist in less than ten days
for that Bounty*

*I think the Rebbels are getting pretty well drubed
out this winter   do you think they will have
to Draft in Poultney and are those exempt that
Paid their three Hundred dollars in the last Draft
would laugh to see Chauncey Maranville traveling
down this way with his gun on his back   I think
men are more apt to Enlist after having been once
in the service   it looks pretty rough to those that
have never been in the army   guess I must close
now   I have got lots of work to do to Day   just
been to Breakfast   ate only six large Potatoes
Appatite very Poor as usual   good bye*

Proctor Swallow

P.S. did you get my letter some time ago wishing you to send me $20   if you did not get that one send it when you get this one   what money I have now I have to hire and give 15 Pay Day for 10 now

dont like that

Yours   PS

Capt Clark has Resigned   I am very sorry   the Company has lost the only Officer there was in the Co that was worth a D—d   I had as go to the D—l now as to stay here   guess we shall go there soon

Your P.S.

Barrancas Fla
Dec 25ᵗʰ 1863

Loomis

There is some men from this Regt going to Vermont to get Recruits   James Oakman is going from this Company   now I wish you would let him have Fifty Dollars that is if it is not going to be to much trouble for you   if it is you need not do it the Reason why I want it is so that he can buy me some Watches   the Watch you sent me I sold for $35   I sent to Clark & Bros for some Watches but they did not send me as good watches into $5 for the same money that you did   I should have

plenty of money but I do not get my Pay until the
Regt gets Paid off which will probably be in Jan or
March   buying Watches for 15 and selling them
for 35 is very good buisiness   I hear that money
was never so Plenty as at present in the North
I am well and hope this will find you all well at
Home   tell Fanny to send me 25 or thirty yds of
that Velvet Ribon such as she sent me last   also
10 yds of the same 2 inches wide and two yds
of cotton Velvet Cloth and four Pair of thick cotton
socks   put them in a small Box and put it in the
Express Office Direct to me Co I 7th Vt Regt Fort
Barrancas Fla via New Orleans   if she has got
any thing good that she dont want she may put it
in   guess that is all   good day   write soon

Proctor Swallow

P.S. wish you merry Christmas

Barrancas, Fla
Jan 31st 64

Loomis

I got my Box today   it came all right but my
Sausage it had burst the can and was hurt   the
Bottles of strawburys were Broken and my can
of maple suggar got jamed but little of it was lost
it got on the Box that had my Shirts in it but the
Paper around it was so thick that it did not get
on any of the things   I guess if you intended I
was going to make all my Brandy into camphire
but the quantity of gum that you sent me I made

a pint of camphire and we have drank the Rest of it   there was a lot of Boxes but mine was the largest one I saw and I think it was the best one we had Pancakes and maple Suggar for supper and are going to have Ham & Eggs for breakfast one of the Boys had a box with a Ham in it   the Eggs came as nice as any thing could be   I gave the Boys a taste of my Cheese and it took half of it   the cookies did not last a moment   they were much better than we get down here   I have sold two pr of suspenders for $2.50 and one pr for $1   that Pays for the whole   I dont know what you think I wanted to do with the Opium   I will tell you   I have always been troubled with the disentery and it will check it the quickest of anything that I can get   if the Regt Re-enlists I shall probaly be at Home this summer and we will make it all right about the Box   by golly it was a good one   when I get Home and you go Soldiering I will send you lots of good things   but I hope that time wont come soon   if I had to Pay for the trouble and for the things that you did not charge me for I think a Box would cost something but never mind $20 a month and no lost time hurrah for Uncle Sam   tell Fanny I did not try on the shirts but they are good ones and when I get Home I will sew for her to pay her for making them tell Mother I am very thankfull for my socks & I guess that is all   good bye   write soon

ProctorSwallow

Barrancas Fla
Feb 14ᵗʰ 1864

Well Loomis

I will write a few lines to you and would send you a Valentine if I could get one   we listened to some Remarks made by our Col this morning on Re-enlisting   if we Enlist before the 1ˢᵗ of March we get $402 Bounty and a furlough of 80 days within the state some time within the present Year would try to get it some time within the first six months   the Officers are all in for it   they know D---d   well that they will have to hoe for their grub   they can sit from morning until night and get $100 per month and they cant get it at Home I have had some thoughts of trying it but have concluded to see them all in H--l and far beyond Horse Heavens and then I wont   not that I have anything in Particular against soldiering but I dont like the style of the thing   I wish to be my own boss for awhile   we have got some Recruits from Vt   our Co got 18   I have got some Vt money $15 if it is good keep it   if not send it back   tell Fan my Shirts are the best fit I ever had and everything else was good but the Honey and I have not opened that   write soon   good bye

Proctor Swallow
P.S. I may change my mind in regard to Enlisting it will depend on how many of the Co does but I dont think I shall   P.S.

Barrancas Fla
February 15ᵗʰ 1864

Loomis

take my pen in hand to write you a few lines   I am well and hope this will find you all well at Home put a letter in the Office for you yesturday   when I wrote it I did not think I should Enlist again but the Company have nearly all Enlisted and I did not want to be the last one   I have Considered the matter over and think it is the best thing I can do   if the War is over in a year it is the best thing to do   if it should last 3 years I should be back again   we shall be at Home some time this year on a Furlough   I presume it will be in June July or Aug   besides I can be detailed as a Tailor by exchanging a Corporals birth for that of a Private and will have no Duty to do and I can get a living here and I never could at Home   Mother could not be any better off if I was at Home than she is now   I hear that the President has called for 500,000 more men   if he gets them I think the south cannot stand it a great while longer   I hope you will be so lucky as not to be Drafted   I hear we can have $125 from the State instead of that $7 per month   I think I had better take that   what do you think about it write and let me know   make a good lot of maple Suggar and grow some Buckwheat so I can have some Pancakes when I get Home   give my love to mother and the children   write soon   good bye

Proctor Swallow

Barrancas Fla
*March 4*th *1864*

Loomis

*I take this oppertunity to write to   I am well
and hope this will you all well at Home   I have
concluded to commute my State Pay of seven
dollars per month and take the State Bounty of
one Hundred and Twenty-Five dollars offered by
the State   so if I should get shot soon I should
get the start of them   if the Power of Attorney
whish you have will draw the money I want you
should draw it   if it wont let me know and I will
send you something that will   it snowed here
a little Feb 25*th   *the only snow we have seen
this winter and we could hardly see that   we
have got 110 Recruits in the 7*th   *they arrived
Feb 18*th   *Co I got 20   there is only one that I
ever saw before   that is Pharsellous Broughton
of Hampton N.Y.   there is a number of men from
Danby Vt   Judge M.H. Cook for one   they are
all good fellows   I guess I shall come Home and
help you do your Haying this summer   give my
respects to all   good bye   write soon*

Proctor Swallow

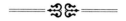

Barrancas, Fla
March 22nd 64

Friend Loomis

I recieved your letter of Feb 8 today   also one from Mother & Fan of a later date containing Mothers picture   you said you had seen James Oakman and gave him $45 but was a little suspicion that I would not get what I wanted   well I dont know as I should but if I dont I must do the next best thing which will be to get it when I can   I suppose I am entitled to a Town Bounty for I have gone to help fill the quota of Poultney   if ther is any such thing as getting a Town Bounty I want you to get it for me   I think I shall be in Vermont before July 1st   tell Fanny to wait until I get Home and then we will get something to put on Mothers floor I had a letter from Henry Lang   he is well   good bye

Proctor Swallow

Barrancas Fla
March 27th 64

Loomis

I thought I would write you a few lines as there is a Boy from this Co going directly to Vermont   I am enjoying good Health   hope this will find you all well at Home   there is no news here

*of importance here   I got the letter you wrote
stating you paid Oakman $45   I have not seen
any Watches   if he has not sent them I do not
want he should now for I dont know how soon we
shall leave here for Vt   we are going to have a
Furlough sometime this Year without doubt but I
dont know how soon   if you have not sent the
things that I wrote for when Oakman went Home
you may wait until you hear from me again*

*I shall send this by Harry Guilder and I have made
arrangements with him to Pay you fifty $50.00
for me   if he does you will please write me   I
want you to tell me if Poultney is going to give
Veterans any Bounty   some of the Towns are
paying a Bounty of $8.00 to those that Reenlist
If Poultney dont give anything I shall go to fill the
Quota of some town that does   give my respects
to all   good Bye*

Proctor Swallow

*Barrancas Fla
April 8ᵗʰ 1864*

Friend Loomis

*I received your letter of March 21ˢᵗ last Night   was
glad to hear that you was all on Earth   I am well
and hope this will find you all well at Home   you
in speaking of my State Pay of 7 dollars said you
did not know as it was continued   well I know
that it is and I have Commuted it and consented
to receive the Bounty of $125 in stead and have*

sent on papers to that Effect and I suppose the money will soon be it is not all ready subject to my Order   now I want you to see if the Power of Attorney will draw the Money   if it will I want you to draw it and use it   that is if you want it   if you cannot draw it I guess you had better wait until I get Home which will be sometime this Summer   the weather is colder here than it was last Year at this time   the two Companys here in the Redoubt have got a garden of about half an Acre of ground fenced in   there is a good many things up large enough to hoe   I guess it will not amount to much as the land here is good for nothing but to raise Water Mellons   Snakes and Alligators   I had a letter from Grove last week   he advised me not to Enlist until I had been Home   when we Enlisted we supposed our time was not out until Feb 1865 but now it seems that it is out in June 1864   some of the men are feeling somewhat grouty about it   if they had known that their time was out in June not a man would have enlisted   the Col told the men very plainly that those who did not Reenlist would not go Home   now they think he deceived them and if it proves true and the oppertunity should ever present itself there is men who would not hesitate to get Revenge   as for me I am not particular providing they do not discharge me before my time is out   I have not heard from Oakman yet   I dont want him to send me any Watches now for I might not get them   I guess there is no danger of him sending any   A squad of 36 Cavelry went out on a Scout the other day and fell in with about 90 Rebel Cavelry   they had a fight   We killed 5 or 6   took 10 or 12 Prisoners and a Lieut without

the loss of a man   these Duck are Devils to fight
give my respects to all   good Bye write soon

Proctor Swallow

Fort Barrancas
May 5th 64

Friend Loomis

I recieved your letter of April 10th last Night   was
glad to hear that you was all well   it found
me well also   I wrote in my last letter that we
were going up the Red River   well we did not
go   the order was countermanded   I think we
shall be Paid off soon and get our Furlough   but
if we should not get it this Year we shall not have
so long to stay after we get back   thats some
consolation   I suppose you will get things fixed
up so nice that shall not know where to stop if I
should come Home   there is no news   Black
Berries are ripe   we have got Turnips in our
Garden as big as a small Babys Head and Green
Corn   also Devlish green to   if I dont get Home
by strawbury time I want you to buy 20 bush and
dry them   I am glad to hear from the money I sent
you to build Barn   I was anxious about it   I
intended to send a Hundred but I found I had not
it so I sent what I had   my Respects to all   good
Bye

P. Swallow

Map of the Gulf

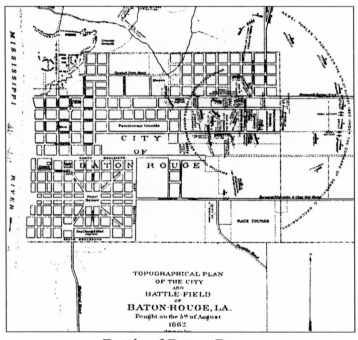

Battle of Baton Rouge

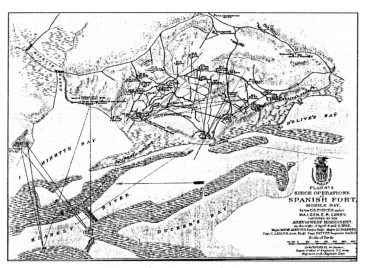

Map of a Spanish Fort

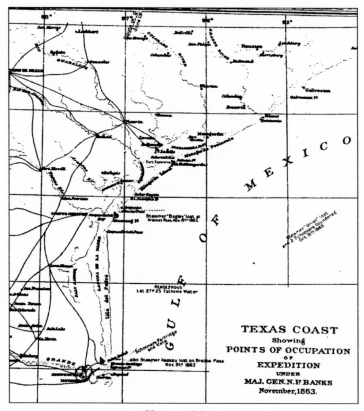

Texas Map

A redoubt at Fort Barancas near Pensacola,
Florida.

Mustering Out at Battleboro

This currency was issued by the City of Baton Rouge in 1862 prior to its capture by the Union forces

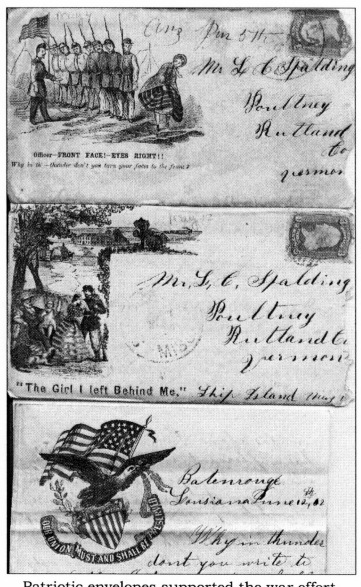

Patriotic envelopes supported the war effort.

Barrancas Fla
May 18th 64

Loomis

I take this oppertunity to write you a few lines   I am well   hope you are all well at home   I have not heard from you in some time   I send by express to day   Two Hundred and Fifty dollars $250   please write me as soon as you get it the Agt who came here from New Orleans is from Middletown, Vt   his Name is Loomis   he told me that you were his Cousin   he sends his respects to you   in regard to my coming Home you may look for me in about Twenty Days after I start from here   when that will be I cant tell   the Regulars are ordered from this place to the North   two Companys of the 7th is going into Fort Barrancas and two more into Ft Pickens   the remaining two Companys have charge of the Batterys   Co I remaining where they are   if the Boys have any strawberries to sell buy some and Dry them for me   do you know what has become of Oakman you may think I am Disappointed in not coming Home but I dont care how long they wait if they let us remain where we are   it is a fine Place   give my love to Mother and the Children   write soon Good Bye

P. Swallow

Barrancas
May 23rd, 1864

Loomis-

Enclosed you will find an Order for $125　　by
Presenting it to the State Treasurer you can draw
the money　　if it will not draw the cash you will
keep the order and write to me　　if you get the
money let Fanny have what she wants to use of it
she said a while ago she was going to get Mother
a Carpet　　if you dont get it let her have some
of the money I sent　by Express　　tell her to buy
me all the strawberries she can get　　I have not
heard from you in some time　　I hear they have
had a big fight at Richmond　　give my love to all

good bye

Proctor Swallow

Fort Barrancas　Fla
June 4th, 64

Friend Loomis

I take my Pen in hand to write you a few lines　　I
recieved your letter of May 15th last Evening　　was
glad to learn that you was all well　　I am enjoy-
ing the best of health　　I hope when I hear from
you again to hear that　Gen. Grant is in Richmond
you think it is rather Doubtful about the 7th Regt

*getting a Furlough   well I dont know but it is
however I dont care about getting to home before
the first of Sept and I shant make any fuss if I dont
get it then   not that I dont want to come home
but we have got a good place here   better than
we shall get again soon   you said Guilder had
not Paid you any money   well I suppose he has
found ways for his money but never mind   he
may want to get accommodated again some time
I hear that James Oakman is in New Orleans   I
guess my $45 has gone to the Devil*

*I sent you by the last mail an Order on Vermont
State Treasurer for $125   we can get green Peas
Cabbage New Potatoes and Black Berries string
Beans down here now by Paying a very hand-
some Price for them   dont be afraid to write for
I shall be here for some time yet I presume   give
my love to Mother and the Children   good bye*

*P. Swallow
Barrancas, Fla
June 19 (64)*

Loomis

*I take this oppertunity to write you a few lines   I
am well and hope this will find you all well at
Home   James Oakman has got back to the Regt
he brought me lots of Watches   if I had many such
chaps to deal with I should get Independently Poor
Guilder has got back also   he did about as well
as Oakman but that is all right   he did not get
his Pay as he had expected   he is an honest boy
so I shall get it some time   I see by the papers
that Grove Scribner is wounded   I dont expect*

*to come Home now in some time   perhaps not
till the War is over   who are you going to have
for the next President   I have not desided yet
which is my man   Lincoln or Fremont   if this
Rebelion   is not crushed or as good as put down
by Nov   I think Fremont is the man to finnish it
write often   good bye*

Proctor Swallow

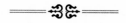

*Barrancas
June 20ᵗʰ 1864*

Loomis

*I have this evening recd a letter from you with $10
stating that you had sent me my Box   I dont know
whether there is any Express on board or not but
shall know tomorrow   it will be six weeks day after
tomorrow since we had a mail   the longest we have
ever been   I should have wrote before if there had
been any chance to send a letter   I am glad you did
not send any more money for we was Paid the 15ᵗʰ
I intended to send Home $50 but there is no chance
to get it to the Express Office   last Fall there was an
Express Agent here with the Pay Master   I did not
wish to risk it by mail   so I have lent most of it   get
50 per cent til next Pay Day   if I had got your letter
a few days sooner I would have held on to it   but I
suppose it wont come amis next Pay Day   I hope
you wont get Drafted & think the People of Poultney
were short sighted   they should know that men
would not Enlist for $300   when other towns were
paying 500   well I will adjourn until tomorrow*

Jun 21ˢᵗ

*My Box did not come on this boat   guess it will
be here on the next one*

good bye

Proctor Swallow

*Barrancas Fla
June 25ᵗʰ, 1864*

Friend Loomis

*I take this oppertunity to inform you that I have
recieved your letter of June 8ᵗʰ   was glad to hear
that you was all well   my health is good   the
weather is fine but very warm   Fanny said she
hoped I would get my Furlough soon   I think the
chances are small for getting it in less than two or
three months   the men who did not reenlist were
to be Discharged the first of June but they are not
Discharged yet   I dont know why they are kept
the Yellow Fever has made its appearance in the
Navy Yard at this Place   such is the report today
I hope it is false   it is to early for it to appear
you said that Grove was coming Home as soon
as he got able   give him my respects if you see
him   give my love to Mother and Fanny   Fred
and Albion   I must close   Good Bye   dont be
afraid to write   I shall be here some time yet*

Proctor Swallow

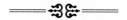

Barrancas, Fla
July 29ᵗʰ, 1864

Friend Loomis

Dear Sir

I take this oppurtunity to write you a few lines   I
am well and hope these lines will find you all well
at Home   it is a long time since I have heard from
you   I sent you two hundred and fifty dollars
the 18ᵗʰ of May but have not heard from it yet   I
also sent you an Order on the State Treasurer for
one hundred & twenty five dollars and have not
heard from it   I dont know but you are waiting
to have me get my Furlough   if so you need not
wait any longer for I am not going to have any   I
guess they would like to have the men Reenlist
again   the thing is just here the Colonel told
the men that their time was not out until Feb 1865
but as soon as the Regt had Enlisted then their
time was out in June 1864 and most of them are
talking Big   I think that one half of them would
shoot the Col if they should have a fair chance
as for me I should not Reenlisted if I had known
my time was out in June   but they only fooled
me 8 months and as for a Furlough I should like
to come Home but I dont feel so bad about it as
the most of them do   if I dont get Home in a
year I shall have the less time to serve when I get
back   if I cant come before cold weather I rather
wait til another Summer   there is a rumor that
Gen Grant is killed   I hope it may prove false   I

suppose you are having considerable talk about a President   we dont get papers here to get much news until 5 or 6 weeks after everybody is dead   I think from what I can hear by the by that Fremont has cut a big Pig in the _____ and I dont think he can be President   I should not vote for him if I had a chance to vote   six months ago I should gone for him   the Gen and between me and two thousand men Black & white went out on a scout last week and was gone 4 or 5 days   they captured 9 or 8 Rebs and a part a musket   the men in this Regt that did not Reenlist have not been Discharged yet but I think they will be soon   I have two of the men orders on you   one of Thirty & one of Twenty dollars if they see you before I do and they very likely will I wish you would Pay them   give my love to Mother and all the rest of the children and dont be afraid to write for I may not be at Home in six months   I must close now

Respectfully Yours
Proctor Swallow

NINE
FURLOUGH AND NEW
ORLEANS

The long-awaited furlough finally came through and the members of the Seventh Regiment who had re-enlisted boarded the Steamer *Hudson* for the trip north. It took ten days to reach Fortress Monroe in Virginia and the ship stopped there to load coal. When the doctor at the fort learned they had come from Pensacola, he threatened to quarantine them for thirty days for Yellow Fever. This would-be disaster was cleverly averted by a technicality. Once the coal was loaded, the Colonel (who <u>had</u> heard the orders to remain) declared himself sick and Lt. Colonel Peck (who <u>had not</u> heard them) took over and gave orders to leave immediately. It took three or four more days to get to New York City and they boarded a train there for the remainder of the journey to Brattleboro. Governor Smith and the townspeople turned out to greet them upon arrival on August 26.

The men were furloughed for thirty days and journeyed on to their respective homes. They reassembled in Brattleboro on September 27, departed by train on the 30th, and arrived in New York on October 1. They embarked on the ship *Cassandra* which left on October 4th. They sailed past Pensacola where they had spent much of the past two years and returned to New Orleans on October 13th.   A cotton press on Annunciation Square provided quarters for the unit.   The soldiers were drilled in street maneuvers and firing and performed guard duty.[27]

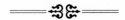

Sept 29 (64) Brattleboro   Vermont
Friend Loomis

I now take my pen in hand to fulfill the promise I made you when I left you   I think we shall Leave here tomorrow   give my love to all   Loomis I am going away feeling worse than I ever felt before.   Loomis I have been a wild Boy but I have not been in the habit of abusing any one worse than I did myself   now I have abused the best Girl that ever lived   I did not know how much I thought of that Woman til I had to part with her I never lived two months that seemed as long as the last two days has   but it is my own falt   I have no one to find any falt with but myself   but there is one that has suffered for me   but if she has suffered more for two days than I have and I have been the cause of it   I have little reason to expect forgiveness   but I do ask for it and hope it may be granted   I can write no more and if you dont hear from me again in four days I want you to write to me and Direct to Proctor Swallow Co I 7th Vt. Vet. Vols. New Orleans, LA   when you answer this I wish you would ask Fanny Stephen if she will not write me a few lines   if only a *few it would be the greatest pleasure she could bestow on me   Adieu for the present*

Proctor Swallow

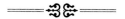

New Orleans
Oct 14th 64

Friend Loomis

I arrived here yesterday at 4 PM   9 days sail from New York   the quickest trip we ever made and as far as good health and fine weather could make it was a pleasant one   Mr Giddins who enlisted in East Poultney Died on the Passage from N.Y to N.O   I did not learn the cause of his Death Billy Miller and Dan Ensign did not come with him they were left at New Haven Ct   the 7th came on the Steamer Cassandra   we are on board of her yet   where we are destined to go I cant tel but there is two Regts of troops in the City whose term of service is out and I presume we shall be kept here in their place for the Present   but I hope not for I have got sick of City life   besides this is a miserable Lousy hole   as soon as I get settled down in some place I will write again   give my love to all   Adieu

Proctor Swallow

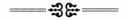

New Orleans La
Nov 13ᵗʰ 1864

Friend Loomis

I think I can spend a few moments to no better purpose than writing Home   I am well and hope these few lines find you all well at Home   there is no news here worth mentioning   how is it in Poultney   how did Election go   did you Elect Old Abe and what did little <u>Mac</u> say when he found it was no go for him   I see by the Papers that you have had a Raid in Vermont[28]   did you get my Satchel and Pants that I sent Home from Brattleboro   I have been working at a new trade for a few days   post Carpentering   this Regt is stationed in a cotton Press with nothing but sheds with Bunks in them for Quarters   four of us have bought stuff and built us a room   got a Stove in it   it is a fine Place for winter   what do you think about letting me have 10 or 12 Pounds of Butter and a small cheese   if you have got time to do it   I would like to have you send me a Box   I dont care for anything but some Butter & cheese unles mother has got some dried Berries that she dont know what to do with   how does the little shaver get along and what is his name[29] I suppose he is one of the finest Boys in the State give my love to Mother Fannie and Fred and all the rest   write soon   give us all the news

Yours sinc
Proctor Swallow

New Orleans La
Nov 20th 1864

Friend Spaulding

I have just received a mail from the North   two letters from you mailed in Aug & July and one from Grove Scribner when he was at Burlington and one from a friend in Poultney Nov 7th the only one of any later date than Sept   but I suppose I can answer them as well as though they was mailed in Nov   I have had no letters from you since I left home   Fannie[30] informed me that you had got a young sonny at your House   the weather is fine here   I think it will be cold enough soon we have had no frost but once this fall and then it could hardly be seen   I see that Lincoln is elected President and that the Union forces are every day gaining some victory either by land or Water   but I will not try to tell you any news as the news that we get here comes from the north so you get it long before I do   give my love to Mother Fanny and all others who may enquire   hoping this will find you all in as good health as it leaves me   I will close   I shall be very happy to hear from any of you when you can make it convenient to write

From your
Obt. Servt.
Proctor Swallow
Company I
7th Vt. Vet. Vols.
New Orleans
Louisiana

P.S. I wish you would go to some of the Teachers in Poultney   I presume the Commercial School would be the Place to go and get me some Books   I want to study Book Keeping as I have considerable time that I think would be spent to a better advantage if I spent them studying than at any other purpose You can find out what I want by enquiring of some teacher   I dont know what they will cost or do I care providing I get them   if you get this in time you can send them in my Box   send a Bill of cost with them   good bye

Proctor Swallow

New Orleans, La.
Nov 28th 1864

Loomis

Your letter of Nov 12th is at hand and was glad to hear from you and to learn that you was all well at Home   I am as well as usual or as well as could be expected for a man of my age   there is no news worth mentioning   the weather is pleasant and warm   I am enjoying myself very well this winter   I have hardly been out of

Quarters since we came here what leasure time I have I spent studdying   I have got quite a Library of Book   do you think I can <u>Lie</u> fast enough to be a good Lawyer   you say you have seen the Selectmen about the Town Bounty and they do not see fit to Pay it   I did not suppose they would until it had been voted on again   I think it might be laid before the Town at their meeting on March next   ask John Beaman what he thinks about it   Fannie says you talk of selling your Farm how is it   do you think the Rail road will go through your Farm   if it does and you can sell your Farm for Slating Purposes you will do well as for the Two Hundred Dollars you wished me to send you I am sorry to say I cant accommodate you at Present as we have not been Paid off since last April   when we get some money I will try and send you the required sum   I expected to be Paid before now and I am about out of money myself   give my Respects to all   good bye
         P. Swallow

         New Orleans, La
         Dec 11ᵗʰ, 1864

Friend Loomis,

I will write you few lines not however in answer to any that I have received from you of late for I have recd none but am in hopes of hearing from you at some future day   I am enjoying good health and am Happy as plenty of good <u>Mule Meat & Hard Tack </u>can make a man   the weather is somewhat colder than it has been but we have plenty Wood and a good Stove and are waiting Patiently for <u>Peace</u>   which I suppose we will have when somebody whips the Rebs   I have heard that John Beaman is dead and I wish you see Henry Clark or some other good man and see if that Bounty affair cannot be laid before Town at their meeting in March   there must be a time when it can done and be legal   I would like to know if they are going to pay it or not   I wrote to you for some Butter & Cheese   I hope you will send it for we have not been Paid in seven months and money has nearly played out and we are living poor   I think I should have starved outright if my Bunkmate had not had a Box from Home   since I left Home and good things are not to be had I have had a ferocious appetite   I have often heard People say they could eat a Nigger Funeral Corps and all, if my appetite continues to increase I dont know what I may be tempted to do   I am in hopes to get my Box before I have to resort to Cannibalism   I think I could eat a white nigger with a good will but these around here are so <u>pesky Black</u>   I suppose you are having plenty Snow in Vermont now   I have not seen any Snow in so long I hardly know how it would look   in fact I have little desire to see any Snow I must close   give my respects to Mother   Fanny and all the Children   write soon

Proctor Swallow
Co I 7ᵗʰ Vt. Vet. Vols.
New Orleans, La.
Dec 11ᵗʰ 1864

———❧———

New Orleans, La.
Dec 17ʰ, 1864

Friend Spaulding,

I address you for the Purpose of giving you my compliments informing you of my good health and obtaining a favor   I wish to get $55 Fifty five Dollars of you until I get Paid   enclosed is a bil of traps that I would like to get if I can without being any trouble to anybody   I dont think I shall want the money longer than Jan next and if it is not convenient for you to let it go   you will not do so as it is only a little speculation to make a few Dollars without work   if you can spare the money you will enclose it in the envelope with the Bill of stuff required and put it in the Express office, pay the Express on it and oblige

Very Respectfully,
Your Obt. Servt.
Proctor Swallow
P.S.   if you send the money send it immediately so I can get the things before or by the middle of Jan

Yours Proc Swallow
My respects to all enquiring friends

Dec 27th 1864

Friend Loomis,

Your letter of Dec. 15th came to hand this evening was recd and read with pleasure   am glad to hear that you are all enjoying good health as well as myself   you have not told me what the Babys name is or perhaps you will not give him any name   I understand there has been or is to be another call for 300,000 more men   are you going to Pay Bounty or Draft   I think a Draft will be the cheapest for you but might not be the pleasantest for some of you   how is it about the Malitia   if you enlist in that can they Draft you I dont hear anything about your selling your Farm lately   have you concluded not to sell it   there is no news here   if you have any lets have it give my respects to all   write soon and often

*Yours Respectfully
Proctor Swallow*

*New Orleans, La
Jan 2nd 1864 (5)*

Friend Loomis

I take this oppertunity to write you a few lines   I am well   hope this will find you all well at Home the New Year has commenced very pleasantly   I hope it will continue so we have good news from the North

Sherman has captured Savannah   Thomas has cleaned Hood out & &   I think the present year may end this war   I hope so at all events what do you think about it   the weather is very pleasant here   it is like Sept in Vermont   to day is fast day here   the Men are all out in the Park playing ball   I have but little desire for such sports since I got to be old and infirm or perhaps I am too lazy   are you going to let them Draft you this time   if you do come into the 7ʰ Regt and I will learn you the Tailors trade   I should not be surprised if this was the last call they will make for men   I am daily expecting my Box   wont I get fat when it does come   guess I must close give my respects to all   write soon

Your Obt Servt
Proctor Swallow
Company I 7ʰ Vermont Vet Vols
New Orleans, La
Jan 2ⁿᵈ 1965

New Orleans La
Jan 19ᵗʰ 1865

Friend Loomis

Your letter of Jan 4ᵗʰ is at hand   it found me in good health   I am sorry to learn that the babys health is so poor but as he grows older he may improve in health   the Box you sent me all come in good shape   the Box part was pretty well used up but the Iron held it together   the North East corner of my cheese got slightly disfigured but not to hurt it   the other things was all right   the Books you sent me are very nice   I am highly pleased with them   tel Fred[31] I got the big Potatoes he sent me will have them for Dinner and thank some one very much for some walnuts Berries Sausage Cake & &   every thing is very exceptable for the reason that we have no money to buy anything   we have not ben paid yet and I dont know as we ever shal I must close   give my love to all

Adieu for the present   write soon

Proctor Swallow

New Orleans La
Jan 31st 1865

Friend Spaulding

Your letter of Jan 16th is at hand   every thing is lovely   I have not got the things   I went to the Express Office to day but the Express had not been got of the Boat   I presume it is there   when I sent for it I thought we should be Paid before now but have not been and if anybody knows when we are going to be they are ahead of my time   as near as I can learn the reason why we dont get Paid is this   when the Estimate was made of the amount of money it would require to pay the Troops in this Department up to the first of Jan this Regt. was not included as we were not here   had not returned

from our Furlough   there was Six Millions of Dollars
sent here in Dec but it required it all to Pay the other
Troops   so the prospect is very poor of getting any
money at present   how are you getting alone with
your Quota   give my respects to all the folks   I
must close   write soon

> *Yours & &*
> *Proctor Swallow*
> *Company I 7ʰ V t Vet Vols*

> *New Orleans Louisiana*

The Books you sent me are very nice but there is
some parts of them that would bother a Philidelphia
Lawyer to see into   but any way to kill time

> *New Orleans La*
> *Feb 12ᵗʰ 1864 (5)*

Loomis

We are going into active service and are packing
our traps   I dont know where we shal go to but
think we may go to Mobile   we may go into Camp
at Camp Parapet for a few days   when we get
in Camp I will write again

my love to all

> *Good bye*
> *Proctor Swallow*

TEN
MOBILE

Admiral Farragut closed the last major port on the Gulf Coast when he defeated the Confederate fleet operating out of Mobile Bay. By the end of the battle all the Rebel ships had been sunk, run aground, or surrendered. The navy then began clearing the bay of torpedoes. The capture of the city of Mobile awaited only the decision to attack the several forts protecting it.

That job was given to Major General Edward R.S. Canby and he began assembling a task force with troops brought from Pensacola and New Orleans. The Seventh Vermont Volunteer Regiment embarked on the steamer *Clinton* on February 19, 1865 arriving at Mobile Point on the 21. It was assigned to General Benton's Division of the Thirteenth Corps. Because action was imminent, the baggage allowance was minimal limiting each soldier to one suit, a change of undergarments and an extra pair of shoes. Coats were not allowed. Only shelter tents were issued and sutlers were excluded. Rations were confined to hard tack and salt meat and troops were instructed to keep three days cooked rations on hand. Camping in shelter tents on barren sand during the storms of February and March was misery and no one was sad when the orders came to break camp early in the morning on March 17.

They marched thirteen miles and camped at Bayou Portage. Torrential rains the next few days impeded progress. The swampy ground, described as 'a mere crust covering a bottom- less quicksand', made it necessary to stop and corduroy the roads. Then the 'corduroy' began to float. Every wagon team was mired. Confederate cavalry harassed the advance guards. Finally, on March 23, they were again on a good road and marched six miles, crossed the Blakely River on a pontoon bridge, and come into camp. That night when the bands played *Oh, Aren't You Glad you're Out of the Wilderness* it had special meaning for the beleaguered troops. Canby's assault began on March 25, 1865 at Spanish Fort on the east side of the Bay led by General Benton's Division. By the end of the next day they were within three miles of the fort. Assault lines formed the fol- lowing morning and sharp skirmishing began. The men of the Seventh were midway between Spanish Fort and Red Fort and within 600 yards of the earthworks of that fort when they halted. All day they lay under a heavy raking fire from the guns of Red Fort as they awaited an order to assault the works. For the next several days and nights, companies took turns relieving each oth- er in the trenches sleeping in the mud. Though constantly exposed to artillery and musketry fire there were few casualties.

A flotilla under Rear Admiral Thatcher arrived to support the siege of Spanish Fort and the army continued to inch closer to it each day. Finally, the Confederate defenders surrendered to the inevitable on April 8. Five thousand prisoners and huge amounts of ordinance stores and guns were taken. Fort Blakely and Fort Alexis, the other key defenders of the city, surrendered as well.

On April 9, the same day that Grant and Lee were meeting in Appomattox Court House, the Washington newspapers reported: "Our troops have entered Mobile and are this evening in full possession...."[32]

Camp near Fort Morgan
Feb 23ʳᵈ 1865

Loomis

Having a few leasure moments I will write a few lines   we left N. Orleans the 19ᵗʰ   the place we are in resembles Ship Island the nearest of any place we have been since we left there   White sand   we are in what they call <u>*Tents*</u>   *each man has a square piece of cloth three feet square four of us button our pieces togather and make a shanty about as large as a Hen Coop   when we move each one takes his House on his Back we are going to call on Mobile in a few days   it has rained every day since we left New Orleans when we left I sent all my Books and other traps to Shrewsbury Vermont in a trunk one of the Boys sent Home   he is a one years man   his time is out next Sept and when he goes Home he can*

send them back to me   I left the City before my
things got there from New York   guess they
have gone up   we got our Pay just as we ready
to leave   they did not dare to pay them before
there is a part of the men that act so bad when
they get money that they dont like to pay them
til they got ready to leave   about one Hundred
run off and got left as it was   every boat that
arrives from N.O. brings a squad of them   I had
no chance to get to the Express Office so I guess
I will keep what money Ive got til I come around
again if the Rebs dont get me   I have to set on
the Ground cross leged and write on nothing   I
must close   write soon

Direct to New Orleans

Proctor Swallow

Mobile Point Ala
March 5th 65

Friend Loomis

I think I will write you a few lines being about
to leave our present Camp for some unknown
place   I have recd no letter from you since I left
N.O.   my health was never better   I think I can
stand a long march   we have got some Recruits
from Vermont   Edward Vaughan and a Boy
by the name of Persons from Poultney are in our
Company   we are getting along very well here
there is plenty of fresh Fish and Oysters here   I
am going to cook the last of my Berries for supper

tell Fred I found his <u>big Beans</u>   we got no news here so I have none to send you   give my love to all and if I dont get <u>kilt</u> I will write again some time

Direct to New Orleans

Proctor Swallow

Mobile Point   Ala
March 11ᵗʰ   1865

Loomis

I enclose your Seven Dollars $7.00   it is some money that I cant use here   if the Five Dollar Note is not good put it in a letter and send it back to me we expect to leave here every day   my health is good   we live on Oysters here   can buy them for a penny a piece as big as a little Dog   we are about thirty miles from Mobile City   the Fleet left here this morning   we can hear them firing I think we shal be off tomorrow or Monday   give my love to all and if I come that way this summer I will call and see you   I have not heard from you in some time   when you get time write to me

Good Bye
Proctor Swallow

━━━ ❦ ━━━

New Orleans La
March 24th 65

Loomis

*Since writing my last letter to you we have
changed our base of opperations   I dont know
where we are (and if you can find out I wish you
would let us know)   we started the 17th and
have marched til to Day   we are waiting for
another Army Corps to join us   shall march
again tomorrow   Mobile seems to be the place
of attraction   but I should not wonder if we went
in that direction til we got near the City and then
take another direction   the weather has been
wet this spring and the Country is low   we
have had to build about twenty miles of Corderoy
Road   my health is good also that of the Regt
the Country so far has been covered with Pine
Timber   have not seen 10 Acres cleared   we
have got the largest Army I have ever seen   it is
Commanded by Genl Granger   our Regt is in the
2 Brigade 3 Div. 13th A.l   I have not heard from
you since last winter   when you get time write to
me   give my love to Mother and all the rest of the
folks   Babys included   I suppose they voted
to Pay me that Town Bounty   how is it*

Proctor Swallow
Directions
Co I 7th Vt Vet Vols
2nd Brig 3d 13th Al

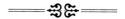

Alabama
March 31ˢᵗ/ 65

Loomis

I have just recd a letter from JB Beaman of Poultney　he informed me that the Town has Voted to Pay me two Hundred Dollars additional Bounty　he also sent me an affidavit to sign that I had not sold or made over my Bounty to any one I signed it but informed him that I had given you the Power of Attorney and told him he had better see you before he presented his papers　and if he drawed the money to retain his Fees and Pay the Balance to you and if you get it I want you to pay him his charges

We are near the mouth of Spannish River　Ala our Forces are about 60,000 perhaps more under Genls A. J. Smith　Granger Steel and any quantity of Brig Genls　Gen Canby commands the whole we have been here five Days　the Rebs have got strong works　Five miles in extent　we attacked them the first day we got here and have been fighting ever since　we shal not be able to bag them til the Fleet can get into Mobile Baby and cut their water communication　we are 12 miles from Mobile　our Entrenchments are　½ mile from the Rebs　we fortify nights and what dont go on the skirmish line stay in the entrenchments days the fighting has been mostly Artilery and Skermishing　our Siege Train has just got here I am under a Breastwork　the Shells and Bullets

are flying   all sorts   we have to releive our
Skermishers after dark   I was on the Skermish
line one day   it is fun to be out where you have
to crawl on your belly and every time you lift your
Head or fire your gun get a Dozen Bullets after
you   I dont know as our Regt has had any men
killed   we have had a good many wounded   I
have been lucky so far   have had no letter from
Home in an age   give my Respects to all   write
soon   Direct to New Orleans

Proctor Swallow
P.S.   Co K was mostly killed and taken Prisoners
on the Skermish line last night

(this was written on the back of the letter from Mr.
Beaman about the bonus

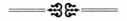

Camp near Mobile Ala
April 16ᵗʰ /65

Loomis

Your letter of Mar 17 is at hand   it found me
well   about the Bounty   I recd the letter from
Beaman you spoke of   I signed the Affidavit and
send it back to him   I wrote to you the same time
telling you if you got the money to pay him his
feels   I told him if he got it to retain his fees and
pay the Balance to you   I thought of sending the
Affidavit to you but did not know hardly what to
do   so I sent it to him   if you had done as he
did, wrote to me ammediately   I should then have

known what to do   but get what you can and hang on to it   it is about as much as it is worth to bother with it   the 13th Al entered Mobile the 13th inst   there was no resistance after Spannish Fort & Blakely surrendered   they had splendid fortifications & very strong but not men enough to man them   the news is very favorable from Grants Army   we are in a small place 7 miles from Mobile   we drove the Rebs out and saved a large Machine Shop and Foundry Steam Mill Car Factory &   give my love to the folks

Good Bye
Proctor Swallow
P.S.   if Peace is declared I intend to come North

Alabama
April 23rd / 65

Loomis

having a few leasure moments I will write to you we are on the Tom Bigbee River   it is quite a large Brook   we are about 30 miles North of Mobile   I think you would like to have an Army Camp in your Neighborhood one Night   first they would take every live Animal within 3 miles of them   then they would take all the Fence in sight for fires   then if the Genl would furnish you a guard you might save your House   if not when the House was nearer than the Fence they would take your House and burn it   they are like a Drove of Geese   Eat all before them and kill

*all behind them   it is just Reported here that Abe
Lincoln has been Shot and from the source it came
we have reason to believe it is true   it is a sad
thing   I think we shall move tomorrow but we
consider the war is about to an end and the last
Rebs we found were seven miles North of Mobile
my Health is good and hoping this will find you all
well at Home   I will close   write soon*

*Your &c
Proctor Swallow
Co I   7ʰ Vt Vet Vols.
New Orleans :La*

*P.S. Strawberries & Blackberries are ripe   I have
not found enough for a Short Cake yet*

Yours   P.S.

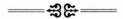

*McIntosh Bluffs   Ala.
May 4ᵗʰ 1865*

Friend Spaulding

*your letter of April 17ᵗʰ is at hand   it found me
in the best of health   I Recd the Five Dollars
you sent   it was a Bill that I bought of one of the
Boys that Enlisted in Poultney at a discount   he
agreed to redeem it if it was not good so I dont
loose anything by it   the Bounty I have given
you instructions about heretofore   I am very
much grieved to learn the People at Home are
sick   I hope they will soon recover   you speak
of planting Potatoes   I intend to be there to
help eat them   things are going about as when*

I wrote you last except   we have mooved a few miles up the River   we are building a Fort here three   U. S. Pay Masters arrived to Day and Regt will get no pay   the Capt lost all of his Muster Rolls   I have got plenty Dash   some of the Boys have had a letter from Josh Baxter   he was at Home on a Furlough   we left him at New Orleans sick   there is a suspencion of Hostilities here until further orders   good   I think of nothing more at present so I will close   write soon   give my love to all

> *Goodbye*
> *Proctor Swallow*
> *Co I 7ᵗʰ Vt Vet Vols*
> *Mobile*
> *Alabama*

P.S.   please find enclosed $5.00 Five Dollars and Cr. my acct

> *Mobile Alabama*
> *May 10ᵗʰ 1865*

Loomis

Dear Sir

having a few leasure moments I will write a few lines to you   we are in Camp just outside the city of Mobile   came down the River yesterday I presume I shal not write again from this place as we in all probability going to Texas to thrash

out Kerby Smith   that is if he dont leave before
we get there   it would please me if he would
surrender before we have drive him out as I am
sick of being a Jack Mule   if we go to Texas   I
may Box up my Over Coat and Express it Home
if I do another man will send some things with me
and I want you to keep them til called for   my
health is excellent   hope the folks are better
than when you wrote last   give my love to all
write soon

> Proctor Swallow
> Co I   7th Vt Vet Vols.
> Mobile Alabama

> Mobile, Ala
> May 12th 1865

Loomis

I send you this Box of things   the Blanket and
one Over Coat and a small bundle marked Albert
Knight Shrewsbury Vermont   I want you to keep
til called for   I f they need airing I wish you
would do it and then take good care of them for
his folks have got my Books to take care of   I
have just got the Box of things from New York   I
got them last night and today I have sold enough
to pay for them and have got enough Brass left to
make a man Poor   there is a number of Negro
Regts here that have just been Paid   I could
not get them in a better time but they played a
little Possum with me   they did not send me so
many Pencils and Watch Chains as I ordered and

in place of them sent four Doz of Boosom Studs and Sleeve Buttons   this is of little account   but I will make something on them for all that   I must close   write soon   give my love to all

> *Proctor Swallow*
> *Co I Vt Vet Vols*
> *New Orleans*

Knights has a Pistol   wish you would oil it and put it away so it wont rust

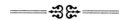

> *Mobile, Alabama*
> *May 25th 1865*

Friend Spaulding,

your <u>rather personal</u> letter of May 7th is at hand it found me well   I sorry to learn that you are all sick but hope the pleasant Summer weather will soon restore you all to good health   I am inclined to think (judging from your last letter) that you are not wholly pleased with the conduct of your Humble Servt.   I am sorry that I have unintentionally offended you   however when you consider the matter over I think you will be induced to overlook past errors as you are aware that it was my sole object to always do right   as for my opinion of J. B. Beaman, it is the same as it was last Fall,   but I was a long way from Poultney and he sent me the Paper advising me to sign it immediately before the Town receded the vote   I did not know but there was some difficulty about the matter and I did not hear from you   I signed *it and sent it to him but informed him that I had already given you a Power of Atty   it was just here   I did not know what to do   I thought of sending it to you as it was and prefered to do so but as I had not heard from you in some time I sent it to him and under the sircumstances I dont think you have any reason to be displeased   as for Henry Clark, Esq.   I am well aware   so are all the rest of the Boys of the influence he used in our behalf and apreciate it   as for yourself and Culver I shall forever hold you in a gratefull Rememberance for the interest displayed on the occasion   the Money you sent to N.Y. I have recd the things and disposed of them at a proffit   I hardly think I shall be Home to help you Hay   but if nothing serious accours   I am in hopes to get Home this Fall*

give my respects to all   write soon

Proctor Swallow
Co I 7th Vt Vet Vols
New Orleans
Louisiana

ELEVEN
TEXAS AND HOME

France attempted to regain possessions and influence in North America while the United States was distracted by civil war and unable to enforce the Monroe Doctrine. Mexico City was captured by French troops in 1862 during an invasion to collect debts. Napoleon III of France installed Maximilian (then archduke of Austria) as emperor. Benito Juarez, President of Mexico, resisted and conflict developed. At the end of the Civil War the United States was ready to re-establish the Monroe Doctrine and the decision was made to maintain a large Army of Observation along the Rio Grande in Texas. Major General Godfrey Weitzel[33] with a force of ten to twenty thousand men was sent to Texas to observe and await the development of the operations of Maximilian and his French allies. The Seventh was one of the regiments designated for this service.

It left Mobile on May 30, 1865 aboard the steamer *Starlight* and proceeded to the lower bay where the unit was transferred to the ocean steamship *Gen. Sedgwick.* It set sail for Brazos on June 2. On June 5 the troops disembarked and went into camp .They remained there until June 14th when they journeyed to a spot near Clarksville about six miles from the mouth of the Rio Grande. They moved again on June 25 to a location nearer the mouth of the river. On August 2nd the regiment marched to Brownsville and went into camp on the east bank of the Rio Grande. About all they had to do was to perform guard and police duty and keep an eye on Maximilian's forces and the Mexicans.

The Emperor's forces had fortified Matamoras and on occasion the Mexicans would lay siege to the place. They never got near enough to suffer seriously from the fortress's guns and the operations seemed 'highly farcical and ridiculous' to the observers. It was suggested that some of the men gained a pecuniary advantage by letting themselves out to fight on behalf of the Mexicans for five dollars a night.[34]

The principal topics of conversation at the camp were wondering whether the Army of Observation would ever move across the river and drive out the Imperialists and when the regiment would be mustered out and they could go home. The second question was answered on March 14, 1866. They were mustered out in place and proceeded as a body to New Orleans and then directly to Brattleboro, Vermont where the regiment was disbanded. The citizens of Brattleboro made a special effort to show their appreciation for the services of the Seventh and held a grand reception for the troops on their arrival.[35]

The Seventh Veteran Volunteer Regiment was formally disbanded on April 6, 1866, a full year after the surrender at Appomattox. All its arms and equipment were turned over to the United States authorities with the exception of that purchased by the men. It was the last volunteer regiment from Vermont to be disbanded.[38]

Brazos Santiago   Texas
June 6ᵗʰ 1865

Friend Spaulding

I write you a few lines not knowing how soon I may have another oppertunity to write again when Texas Surrendered I did not think we should have to come here to Texas but here we are, safe and sound.   I can compare this place to nothing but a Desert   we are going up into the country tomorrow   how long we shall have to remain in this country I cant tell but hope not long   all the water we get is salt water condensed   there is two Steam Engines here at nothing else   the Riogrande River is all that seperates us from Mexico   have some intentions of going there and drive the French & Mexicans out and taking posession   hoping this will find you all well   I will close

Write soon   direct as usual to New Orleans

Proctor Swallow

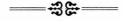

Clarksville Texas
June 24ᵗʰ 1865

Loomis

*your letter of May 25ᵗʰ is at hand   it found me
well   we are Camp on the Riogrande River   can
look over into Mexico   how long we may stay in
Texas is a matter of uncertainty   I hope not long
but presume Vet Soldiers will be held some time
yet.   I am very sorry that you are so unwell at
Home   tell Fannie that I guess she had not better
send me the Babys Picture for I am so far off that
it might not reach me   besides I think moving
around before long   give my love to Mother and
tel her that she need have no fear of my going
to Mexico.   I have got all the Soldiering I want.
am quite ready to come Home as soon as I am
permited to..   there is no news here   give my
love to all   write soon   direct to New Orleans*

Proctor Swallow
Army of the Rio Grande

Clarksville Texas
August 1ˢᵗ 1865

Friend Loomis

*I enclose you an Order for Fourteen Dollars on the
State Treasurer   I wish you would forward it to
the Treasurer as soon as you receive it.   I am a*

little fearful it is to late   but if it does not draw the Money write to me   but if it is because there is no money due to his account you will retain the order about two months and try it again   Williams owed me and I could get nothing else   the Pay Master made his appearence a few days since he was an unexpected but not an unwelcome visiter   he distributed four months pay to this Regt   he came here expressly to pay this Regt   I have had good luck and got all the Money due me but a few dollars   the one years men who were Discharged were oweing me about Sixty Dollars I am looking for it the first Mail   if they did not get it paid in New Orleans they were going to pay to a man in Shrewsbury and I dont know but he will pay it to you   he has his choice to pay it or keep it and have his Brother in Law who is here pay me   it is all safe either way   he is a responsible Man   his name is Albert Knight   he had some things in the Box that I sent you   we have just got orders to move day after tomorrow to Brownsville   I think about 50 mile up the River I understand there is a mail at Brazos   if so I may get a letter from you or some one else   I have got Five Hundred Dollars that I could spare if I had any convenient way to send it   if I get my Money from New Orleans I shall have about Six Hundred and I guess I can contrive some way to get rid of some of it   by the time we get Home or get Paid again if I keep it I can make as much as I shall spend by lending it and I have to do something to get my spending money   I have done no work since we left New Orleans   I had about $300 Three Hundred Dollars when I left there last winter and had $55 worth sent me from

New York and $114 from the Pay Master and if I get my cash from N.O. I shall have $650 besides spending a Hundred or two   if you have got the Recipt that Oakman gave you for that $45 you may destroy it   he paid me last winter

What is the prospect of getting out of this infernal Army   if they dont let me go by next Spring I will desert as shure is faith.   I guess they will let us go before then   there is no news here at all havent seen a news paper in years   well I am not sorry we are going for we can get into no worse place on Earth   well give my love to all the folks and when I get somewhere I will write again

Proctor Swallow

P.S.   the reason why I want you to hurry the order is this   there is another going for another man and I am afraid there is not enough due him to Pay both of them   if there is not the one that gets first is the best fellow &   Proc

I came near forgetting one thing   David B. Hunter informed me that his Mother got Three Hundred Dollars in addition to the one Hundred that he got last fall making Four Hundred in all   I told him I thought he was mistaken I thought they had voted Three Hundred in all instead of Three Hundred in addition to the former one Hundred

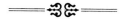

Brownsville Texas
Aug 22ⁿᵈ 1865

Friend Loomis,

*your letter of <u>July 1ˢᵗ or 31ˢᵗ</u> is at hand and found
me well and in Texas   I am very sorry that Mother
is so feeble but hope she will be better when I hear
from her again   I am much obliged to the Town
of Poultney for the very kind favor they have done
me Yes. I am just a Hundred Dollars thankful to
them   yet perhaps I am somewhat indebted to
individual influence but at all events I apreciate
the Hundred Dollars.   I had learned by way of
David Hunter that there was $100 Paid more than
we supposed we should get   however it is all
very well.   there is a little prospect of our getting
Home before long and I for one am not displeased
at the idea of getting out of this <u>Soggering</u> affair.
There is nothing positive about it   some of the
Troops have been mustered out and it reported
that all of the White Troops will be soon.   I took
a short trip into Mexico the other day.   Soldiers
are not allowed to cross the River so we have to
get into a Citizen rig in order to cross the River
when once on the other side of the Rio Grande*

*<u>Uncle Sam</u> lose all his rights & title to us Green
Backs   <u>Poor Fellow</u> is of no account over there
we have to give $10 in US Money for $6 in Specie
Cold Water such as is flowing in abundance in
Vermont is worth <u>or costs</u> 12   ½ cts per Glass
down here_   Northern Potatoes and small ones*

*at that are selling for $25 per Barrel   I little
thought five years ago that I should ever be where
Potatoes & Water would be as scarce as they are
here   you say that Langsyne has Enlisted into
the Regular Army   well if he rather do so than to
work I have no objection   but when I go into the
Regular Army or any other army it will be when I
am Lazier that I am now   and if there is a lazier
Dog on earth than I am show him to me   yet it
is just the life some fellows prefer   I am in hopes
to learn something deffinite about getting out of
Service before I write again   give my love to all
the folks and cheer Mother up all you can as I am
in hopes to be on my way Home in a Month from
this   adieu*

> *From   Proctor Swallow
> Hd Qrs 7ᵗʰ Vt. Vet. Vols.*

> *Near Brownsville Texas
> Sept 14ᵗʰ 1865*

Friend Loomis,

*having a few leasure moments I will write you a
few lines although by good rights you owe me half
a dozen letters.   It is now going on four years
since I have had a letter from you but I am in
hopes to get one soon   I am enjoying good health
and hope this will find you as fortunate at Home
I dont want you to think I am feeling well by a
long Shot for I am Mad yes Mad as   I <u>want</u> to
come Home.   this keeping men down in this part
of the World for nothing is not just what makes me*

feel very good natured but suppose it is all for the best or at least I have been told so by people that I suppose ought to be believed   yet I can hardly swallow it   but if they dont turn me off my next April I shal them   oh dear the Musquitoes are so troublesome   I shal have to adjourn   give my love to Mother and all the Family   I have given up Tailoring   gone to clerking for the Adjutant   dont have much to do but write and not enough of that to hurt myself   if you see Fannie give her my best respects   What has become of Grove Scribner I have not heard from him since he left the Army I will tell   you what it is Loomis   if I was not so provoked about staying down here so long I should get along finely   we can buy Flour Sugar and Potatoes   Onions &c of the Commissary at a very fair price so as to live very comfortable   but I am so fraid they will send us Home.   Well give my love to all and write as often as you can   send all the News

Good Bye
Proctor Swallow

Oh dear I am covered with Musquitoes & Bugs
Musquitoes Bugs Bugs Bugs

Enclosed please find sample if they suit you
on your Order   you may have em or Tick   I
suppose they ought to have a Leg to be knawing
on the route   but guess that they have had nuff
for tonight

HeadQuarters 7th Vt. Vet. Vols
Near Brownsville Texas
Sept 21st 1865

Friend Loomis

I have got a few moments of leasure so I will
write to you and Mother and the Family in general
being in good health having plenty to eat and thats
good to by buying it.   I dont know but I am OK
in every respect but having a desire to get Home
however, I dont know but I shal be as well off here
as I should any where   I have got an Excellent
Situation   my work is easy and neat.   I have

considerable of it to do since I got acquainted with the business.   I have all the Regimental writing to do which I assure you is no small amount but it is just the kind of practice I want   I can I think improve as much in writing here as I could by going to School as was my intention to do this Winter if I had not staid in the Army   I have had no letter from you in some little time   the Mails are very irregular here.   Sept 22nd, 2 o clock A.M.

Loomis before completing my letter yesterday I had some unexpected writing to do which occupied my time until 11oclock last evening   went to bed could not sleep so I will finish my letter.   I have had some inclination to send for my Books   I shall not have much time to study them but evenings if I stay in the Office   but evenings will lengthy this winter and then if we should hapen to go Home but if we should and I should loose them it would not be hard luck on both sides   they are with Albert Knight of Shrewsbury   when he went home he said if he passed through the Town he would call in the latter part of May last   I sent by Addams Express Co a Box containing a Woolen Blanket   a double breasted Cavelry Overcoat a Vest & a Pocket Pistol belonging to him besides an Over Coat Vest and some other articles belonging to myself and as I have never recd my notice from you of your recov it I judge it is lost   I will send you the Receipt if I can find it although I suppos it is of little use   however you might make some inquiries at office in Poultney   the value of the Box was $25.00 but was not stated on the receipt I sent it to the office by the Quarter Master and forgot to state the value   in one of your letters *you informed me that you had got the order for my Town Bounty and that Mr. Beamans charges were $12.00 which is all right and if you did not pay him you may do so at your earliest convenience and charge it to Proc   by the way if Knight has sent my books to you   although I dont think he has   you will do your Humble Servt. A favor by carefully packing them in a Box and forwarding them to Proctor Swallow   Co I   7th Vt Vet Vols Brownsville Texas via Addams Express Co (you understand that is if you have got them) at the same time I am going to write to Knight for them well I guess that is all the business of importance this time.*

end of Volume first   continued volume 2nd concluded

Hold on I forget I must tell you how nice we have got things arranged for boarding which is rather an essential point with me.   You know there is three myself included   that Mess togather   one is a Blacksmith P.A. Brouoghton formaly from Hampton N.Y. (Brother Rumseller) a very fine man. Sold some Rum but guess he never drinked so much of it as I did   he is detailed at Hdqrs has to shoe the Majors Horse occasionaly   the other is a Barber   he is on detailed here   has nothing to do but barber the Officers which is less work than he ever done before for the same amount of pay I guess   well we Mess togather draw our rations and buy what we dont draw enough of   some Sugar fresh Beef Flour Potatoes dried Apples and occasionally at 80 cts. And $1.00 per #pound a little Butter   dont live entirely on Butter mind *you..Beef is the cheapest here of any place we have ever been in Soldiering good steak 10cts pr # at the Market Onions fair size are worth 10 cts each and potatoes and apples are about the same Eggs $3.00 per doz by getting a Commissioned Officer to lie a little and certify that it is for his own use we can buy provision at Commissarys at a fair Price Officers are allowed a certain amount of money to live on and Government furnishes them with Rations at cost prices exclusive of Transportation so by that arrangement they can buy of Govt for nothing compared with other prices Potatoes 2 and 2 ½ cts per pound onions about 3 cts per # Flour 4 ½ &5 cts # Sugar 9& 10 dried Apples 15, so you see the less rations they sell the less transportation for nothing the men with me have so little to do that they do the cooking generally so I have little to do in the <u>Grubb</u> department but to eat my share or as much thereof as I choose you know I am a small eater and I guess you will find some bad spelling here to about that Town Order if you cant obtain the Money on it and if there is no chance for them to rescind the vote or repudiate the debt you might as well get it fixed and have it draw interest if it dont now and keep it well time is precious and I have got another letter or two to write I shall be obliged to ceace writing for this time youl excuse this short letter I will try and write enough more next time to balance whats lacking this time when you write please give me some information respecting Mr. Todds People also Dan Ensign Anson McKilrains Mr. Scribner &c you wont because my message is brief fail to write now if there is any possibility of your being disgusted with a Budget of Nonsense I*

*think Ive got you   the Wolves are Howling   Prairie
things are very purty   they are as fraid of a man
as the Devil is of Holy Water   Roosters begin
to crow and I must go to writing another Letter
give my love to Mother   Fannie   Albion & Fred
and compliments to all who may enquire   Kiss
the Baby for me   Adieu*

Proctor Swallow
Hd. Qrs.   7th Vt. Vet. Vols.

Brownsville Texas
Sept 27th 1865

Friend Loomis

*Your letter of Sept 3rd is at hand   it found me well
as usual but I am very sorry to hear you are so
unwell at Home   but things to day are looking
for the first time in a long while   like getting
out of the service   there is a strong report and I
think there is grounds to believe it true that there
is going to be 20 or 30 Regts mustered out and I
think the 7th will be one of them   I am very buisy
if there is nothing to this I will write again in a day
or two   give my love to all   dont write after you
get this till you hear from me again   Adieu*

Proctor Swallow
Head Quarters 7th Vt. Vet. Vols.

=====☙=====

Near Brownsville Texas
October 8ᵗʰ 1865

Friend Spaulding

Having a few leasure moments I will try and write you a few lines   I have not much to say.   I am some like Jack when he abed had nothing to say) however I am well   yes as tough as a boiled Owl and I hope this will find you enjoying better health at Home than you was when you wrote to me last   in my last letter I guess I told you not to write until you heard from me again as I was coming Home   well dont delay on that account for I am not coming   they were going to discharge a batch of Troops but it proved to Dar Key   I have come to the conclusion that the Seventh will have to stay till the last Dog is hung   I suppose that I could have got a Furlough for Sixty Days if I had tried, as they are giving Furloughs to ten per cent of the men, but I thought it would hardly pay. Although I wanted to go <u>right bad</u> , everything is right good and right smart down here.   Ask a man the distance to any place and will tel you its a <u>right smart ways I recon</u>.   You ought to see the Houses they build down here   about one half of the inhabitants of Brownsville are Mexicans they stick poles in the ground and have them as near togather as they can and then Plaster them with mud.   the covering is in layers like Shingles but thicker and of long grass or straw   they are as ignorant as heathan but I suppose the Poor Devils cant do much better in the building line as

Lumber is worth 25 cts per foot.   I sent by a man that was going to Town the other day to get me two boards five inches wide and ten feet long to make me a bunk.   I sent two dollars and they asked him 2.50   <u>rough aint it</u>   I was telling the Major of it and he says he will get the Quarter master to   make one for him and give it to me. He is one of the best Men out of Jail.   Our Lt Col is absent on a Furlough.   He is a poor piece of property, and we have no Colonel.   I have had tough time for the past ten days   the Adjt went away and it being the first of the month, and the last of a Quarter I had any quantity of Monthly & Quarterly   Returns to make out in addition to every day business.   I have just got everything on the square now, and am happy as a bat in the soap tub   with the usual exception of musquitoes, Bugs &c.   you spoke about money   I am about on a level with that famous <u>Calf of Jobs</u>   you know how poor he was.   I have only $40.00 to my name and I am hanging to that like death to a Nigger.   If I spend that before I get Paid I shal have nothing to buy fodder with   when the Boys went Home on Furloughs they prety much cleared me out.   Broughton one of the men I was messing with has gone Home   the other to his company, so I had to get a new place to Mess my orderly Sergt. that I have always tented with has been Promoted to 1st Lt and I have gone to board with him.   We have two Darkies n the Co and one cooks for him   we have to buy all our grub except coffee and some sugar and salt meat it costs about as much as a man can earn but no decent mans Dog could live on Gov Rations alone. When we were Paid I had $500, that I should sent

Home if there had been any good way to send it
Adams Exp Co have opened an Office since but I
had loaned part of it so I thought I would the rest
if I am as fortunate as I have been it will earn me
as much as my expences will be   but when I get
Paid again I shal send it Home for I should know
it was safe then   and here if a man dies it pays
his debts   there is a man from Wells, Vt. gone
Home on a furlouogh   he is a widower (or what
do you call it) got 3 or4 little children and no wife.
Well he is owing me some over a hundred dollars
and is going to try and get discharged on occount
of his children.   If he does I told him to pay the
Money to you.   he is a good responsible man (or
he would not owed me so much and did not get
Paid last Pay day   it is getting dark and I must
go to supper   give my love to Mother, Fanny,
Albion and Fred. And the Baby   and good Bye

Write soon

> *P.Swallow*
> *Co I 7ʰ Vermont Vet Vols*
> *Brownsville Texas*

> *Brownsville Texas*
> *October 18ᵗʰ 1865*

Dear Mother

As I have not written to you in a long time I will
now attempt to do so   when I write Home I write
to one as much as the other.   If I dont direct to
you I mean you just the same.   I will tell you what

it is Mother   I had got my mind all made up to get Home this Fall but I shall have to give it up I guess.   but if my health is good as it is now I dont but I shall get along as well this winter as I should at the North   I dont mean that I could enjoy myself as well as I could at Home by any means   but I shall have a good position for a Soldier   besides I shall be where I will be improving in what I desire most to learn   my work is all writing and I think it dont average more than two hours per day except at the close and beginning of the Month   then for a few days I am buisy at all hours   but I have to be at the Office all the time as communications are sent in at no stated   time and have to be attended to when they come.   I have a large Tent all to myself and get plenty to eat so you see I am getting along finely   aside from the desire I have to get Home.   but I must close   good Bye

Proc
Head Quarters 7ᵗʰ Vermont Vet. Vols.

Near Brownsville, Texas
November 5ᵗʰ 1865

Friend Loomis,

   After mature deliberation I have come to the following conclusion (that I had better write you a few lines) so here goes.   First, I have nothing to write.   Second, I will write it for I might as well trouble you a few moments as any one else   I am enjoying my usual good health and hope you are all well at Home.   I came very near Perishing *last week with the cold.   it has been very warm all the Fall until about a week ago   it rained and wound up so cold that I thought I should freeze to death   we had no stoves or fire places in the Tents and it was rough I had three Blankets and then I half froze to death   it was not cold enough to freeze or have any frost but I was never so cold in my life   it has come around warm and we have built Brick fireplaces so that I guess we wont freeze anymore   I have been a little effected with the Scurvy not very bad   have got about rid of it   my feet was sore some   but I dont have to travel around any more than I please   I have an orderly at the time to go on errands etc   I dont have to leave the tent for anything but my own personal affairs <u>right smart ha</u>.   Well I guess I am done   give my Respects to any that enquire and my love to Mother and the childrens Fanny and Albion included*

Write soon   Adieu

*   P. Swallow*
P.S.   if you will send me 20 Pounds of Butter in a can and put the can in a Box by Adams Exp Co to Brownsville Texas I will be your Uncle for Ever P.S.

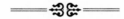

Brownsville Texas
Nov 27ᵗʰ 1865

Loomis

I could not think of retiring this evening without <u>saying good night</u>.   I am well and happy as a clam in the brook   give my love to all   hoping this will find you all in good health   I will say

Adieu
P. Swallow

Brownsville Texas
Dec 12ᵗʰ 1865

Friend Loomis

As the acknowledgment of a letter is so agreable to you I will acknowledge the receipt of yours of the 4ᵗʰ (?) which I received to day   the <u>Skeeters</u> and <u>bugs</u> played out the 1ˢᵗ of Nov when we had a few cold nights.   This is the first notice I have had that you had got the Box of things that I sent last summer.   The single breasted Coat and the dark colored Vest and a pair of drawers and perhaps a pair of socks blonged to me   the Pistol and other things belonged to Albert Knight of Shrewsbury Vt.   the over Coat you or Abion can have to draw wood in if you like   I am glad that you are all as well as you are   Eating trim I suppose is tough and harty   I have lost that ravinous appetite of *mine since I came in the Army and I guess it is a good thing for me to for I have to buy my food or a large portion of it   you cant guess what we had for dinner today   had dumplins and they were lighter than any Canon Balls that I ever saw   but I have seen Dumplins that was lighter   you cant guess who made them.   Well it was Proc and I   you made some remarks about Winchell and Brown   when you write again please inform me if such was the fact and does Brown and his wife quarrel &c   the weather since the 1ˢᵗ of Nov has been pleasant and warm until today   when I awoke this morning the Sun was shining in my face and it was very nice and warm   in an hour from that time it was so cold that I thought I should freeze   I never saw the weather change so quick as it does in this part of the country   I am still in the Adjts Office   our Adjt has been mustered out and the acting Adjt knows nothing about the business in the office and would be to lazy to do anything if he did   I find it is no small job to do the Book of an Adjt and Clerk to   besides I have the Lieut Cols writing to do   I have an Orderly but he does nothing but go on errands   the Act Adjt is also Acting Q/M and is not in the office one in dogs age   the Lieut Col has got his wife with him and is out in a tent by himself and there has to be some one in the office   All the receipts for every thing that is brought in and when   there is an hour or two that I dont have anything to do   I have to stay here and I am getting about tired of it   I told the Col the other day that I would like to go to my company   but it was no go   why   he says   I never had a man in the office that did half as well as you and I believe it to for when I* *came into the office I did not write but little the first month and it took me all the time to pack the papers and &c in some shape so that I could find them without looking all day   I have got so that I know how every thing wants to be done and it is easy work but I dont like to be tied up so clost there is just as much to do on Sunday as any day. I think it is profitable for a man to Keep his family here   our Lieut Col has had his wife here about two weeks and he got a Dar Key that belongs to my company to carry some close (clothes) up town to be washed   he said he carried about one hundred pieces and 17 pairs of stockings   they ask $4.50 a doz for washing and the two weeks amounted to nearly $40.   They say she is very wealthy and I should want her to be.   she was an adopted of Genl John C. Fremont   about that lady you mentioned in your letter   I have the pleasure of knowing her and of knowing that it my acquaintance with her has been of no benefit to me it as sertanly been of no harm and that if her lot is hard   it not because she has merited it   it is midnight   I must retire   give my compliments to all and write as often as convenient*

Adieu from
P.Swallow

Mother

I enclose you my Ambrotype   I had it taken at Mobile   it is not a very good one, but its myself hower and <u>Black</u> as ever   I am stopping in Texas *at present and getting along fine   I have some hopes of getting Home this fall but may not   but a Person does not stand so good a chance to get killed by bullets as he did a year ago   the forces have all surrendered in this before we came here suppose we are here more for observation than anything else   hoping this will find you all well I will close   give my love to Albion   good bye*

From your little <u>Soney</u>
Proctor Swallow
Hd Qrs 7ʰ Vermont Vet. Vols

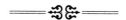

Near Brownsville Texas
January 10ᵗʰ 1866

Friend Loomis

I have a great mind to write you although I have not received a letter from you in some time   I wont write much any how   hold on I will take it back   you are a good boy   going to send me some Butter aint you   I am looking for it every day from long since you sent it   I bought a few Pounds the other day   it was poor stuff however cant expect to get anything very nice for the price   only 1.50 per pound   I dont know as I gave you sufficient authority to send me the butter I believe I told you that I would remember you in my <u>will</u> or something to that effect.   Now if you think that is not going to be worth as much as the Butter I will pay you for it   it is getting so near spring that if you have not sent it before you get this letter you may wait until you hear from me *again. I suppose that I might as well inform you that it is my opinion that I shall remain in service until the expiration of my term of service I have no particular reason for saying so excepting that it is my opinion. I believe that Government is keeping an army here for no other purpose than to agrevate a war with the Imperials. Genl Sheridans orders are such as strictly forbids ought but perfect neutrality he of course receives his instructions from War Dept but I think it is the intention not only of the Comdg Genls but of Gov to furnish the party opposed to the French al the assistance indirectly that they can. When we came here last June it was to quiet the confederates if there was any to be quieted. after they got all the Rebs out of the way what they did they want to bring Pontoon Bridges here for unless to cross the Rio Grande last fall when Mattamoros was beseiged there was plenty of the U.S. Soldiers that went over there and remained a week. And last week Bagdad was captured and there was lots of U.S. Soldiers that participated in its capture they crossed the River from Clarksville where they least expected danger. The comdg Genl has nothing to do with it but if he chose he could very easily prevent Soldiers from going to Mexico but they dont want to do it if the United States wants to drive the French out of Mexico let them raise an army and do it but I dispise the way they are doing now I hope every man that goes there will get his neck stretched I dont know but the Regt will be mustered out in the spring but I dont believe it will I am enjoying good health get plenty of Potatoes and Beef Steak get Potatoes at the commissarys for 3 & 4 dols per bbl and can buy six lbs of Beef steak for 50 cts at the Market   Beef is the article of food kind that is cheap   had a little frost three or four times and a little ice once this winter   there is a great difference in the weather here and at N.Orleans well I must close   give my respects to any of my friends that you see   I dont suppose that my enemys will forget me.   I hear that James Scott is at Home   what kind of chap is he.   Well write and give us all the news*

Yours Adieu
P. Swallow

additonal page with cartoon about drilling for slate enclosed January 10, 1866 letter

=====⚜=====

Camp 7ᵗʰ Vermont Vet. Vols.
Near Brownsville Texas
January 17 /66

How are you my son

*Just recd your or Fannys of Dec 15/65   glad to
hear that you are all kicking about   I am as tough
as a young Injun   recd the letter from Wm. B. Hall
have not recd any before   dont you think Fanny
took the liberty to write a little this time   tel her
she better look out and not to it again   about
money   I have got about 60 cts and 10 of that is
not good   but if I get paid off again I will send
my money Home   Egbert C. Vaughan is going
Home in a few days   I may send a few trinkets
by him   things at present look more favorable
about getting out of service this spring   there
is orders in the Department from Washington to
muster this (White Brigade) out of service and I
hope that the man that hinders us from getting
out will die when his time comes if not before   I
for one have staid here about long enough   well
I guess I will close for this time*

My respects to all

Adieu
P. Swallow
Get some pancakes ready by the time I get home
Proc

Camp 7ᵗʰ Vermont Vet. Vols
Near Brownsville Texas
February 10ᵗʰ 1866

Friend Loomis

Your letter of Jan 6ᵗʰ is at hand   finds me enjoying good health   I have not got the Butter yet but presume it will be here soon   hope so at all events for I want some good Butter   what they have for sale here is musty stuff unfit to be eat 1.25 and 1.50 per Pound at that   you will please accept my thanks until you are better paid   I dont know but I ought to wait until I see whether I am going to get it or not before I thank you to much but I suppose it will not be your falt if I dont get it   so I am <u>yer uncle hereafter</u>   we are having a splendid winter here   the weather is not so cold here as in New Orleans   we have frost but once or four times   I think Brownsville is getting to be the roughest place I was ever in   seldom a day passes without from one to five persons being murdered   the border is infested with a band of cutthroats and Robbers that do nothing but Rob Kill etc   they are a part of the band of the outlaw Cortina   there is no news that I think of at the present time except that I do my own <u>breathing</u>   I guess you would want some one to do your breathing if you had the work to do that   I dont get time to eat but three or four times a day and no time to play   hope to get home soon   there was an order issued for the muster out of this Regt and several others   the order was *issued the 8th of Jan and countermanded on the 9th   I think the Bagdad affair was the cause of its being countermanded   I feel confident that there will be some change by the 1st of April   however tomorrow is my birthday and I will wind up and go to bed so give my love to all and write as soon as convenient*

Proctor Swallow

Brownsville,Texas
March 14th 1866
2 O clock A.M.

Mr. Loomis C. Spaulding

Poultney Vermont

Sir:

I shall be mustered out of service at 9 O clock this A.M. nothing preventing.

Very Respectfully Yours
P. Swallow
Co.I 7th Vermont Vet. Vols.

EPILOGUE

Proctor Swallow was twenty-seven when he returned home after four years with the Grand Army of the Republic. He found room and board with the Stevens family in Poultney and on New Years Day in 1868 married Fannie M. Stevens, one of the daughters. They had no children. For a time, he peddled brooms around the state.

Sadly, the diseases he contracted digging in the swamps of Louisiana plagued him for the rest of his life. Severe diarrhea left him unable to do any kind of hard labor. The problem seemed to be worse in the warmer months and he complained that at times he was so weak he could "not lift a pail of water or an armful of wood". He suffered from severe pain in his back, kidneys, and sexual organs and was unable to lie down. He was "obliged to sleep in a sitting position" most of the time. He fretted that his brain was "muddled" by the continual pain and this prevented him from writing or figuring. Other complaints included cramping and numbness in his legs, a bad blood condition, skin scales especially around the knees, elbows, and breast, a bronze color, and a poor appetite. He sought relief from a series of doctors but nothing seemed to help for long.

His poor health prevented him from returning to his prewar occupation of farming. He moved frequently in search of work and at times lived in Brattleboro and Rockingham, Vermont; Orange and Brookline in Massachusetts, and Torrington, Connecticut. In 1912 he returned to Poultney and remained there for the rest of his life.

When he could, he worked as a bookkeeper, a watchman at a mill, and as a canvasser contracting jobs and hiring men. He had an interest in the manufacture of slates and was in charge of the stationary engine. Each time he thought he was improving, the diarrhea and kidney problems would come back and he would have to miss work and eventually lose the job.

While he was in Orange, Massachusetts, a US Examining Surgeon Dr. Edward Barton suggested he was eligible for an invalid pension. His first Declaration for Original Invalid Pension was filed September 26, 1879 when he was forty-one. It includes supporting letters from officers, fellow soldiers, doctors, and friends. Over the years, he made many more requests for pension assistance and added deafness and loss of teeth to his woes. Eventually he hired the D.C. law firm of Harvey Spalding & Son to assist his case. On May 11, 1912 his pension was $25 a month.

One of the granddaughters of his friend Loomis remembered fondly how he loved children and was always good to them. Each month when he received his pension check he would go into Rutland to get his medicine. As a very young girl, Helen[1] would meet the trolley when he came back and 'march' him down the lane to the house using his cane for a rifle. Her cousin Anna[2] told how he often slipped a candy treat to the children from his pocket. He boarded with her family for a time and she remembers how he was never able to lie down and even sitting in a chair over time was difficult.

Proctor Swallow died on April 19, 1916. It was fifty years after he returned from the war, never again to be 'tuf as a boiled owl.'

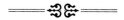

Northfield, Vermont
May 7, 1867

Friend Loomis,

I will write you a few lines   all well and I am going to try and sell some Brooms today. My Brooms got here last evening. I had the express Agt. Telegraph to Burling yesterday morning and they were forwarded. They are a heedless set of fellows   it is raining this morning   give my respects to all   direct a letter to this place which is a very pleasant little village.   I don't want you to say anything but I wish the Brooms were in Tophel   are you going to buy half of my quarry guess you had better   I getting the blues   guess I will go to Australia and dig   Gold

Adieu
Yours Resp
P. Swallow

APPENDIX

The *Baton Rouge Daily News* of Thursday August 7—two days after the battle—contained the following:

Yesterday, the 5th of August, was indeed a day of horror and confusion in Baton Rouge. At about half past 4 o'clock, the rebel troops, under the command of Maj. Gen. Breckinridge and Brig. Gen. Ruggles, attacked the Federal troops here under the command of Gen. Williams, and for the space of more than two hours hailed a shower of shots and bullets into the Federal ranks. Their fire was promptly returned. From a man wounded in this engagement and a member of the Fourth Louisiana Regiment that the force engage under Gen. Breckinridge would probably reach seven thousand men, of whom but four regiments were brought into action.

The U. S. gunboat Arkansas, which was expected to materially aid in the attack on Baton Rouge, did not arrive according to appointment. The U.S. gunboats, five in number, anchored above and below the town, materially assisted in holding the rebel force in check. We have not been able at this writing to gather any information with regard to the Federal killed and wounded but suppose that their loss cannot be more than one hundred total. We passed over the field yesterday after the engagement, and noted some fifteen dead, and probably twice that number of wounded

Confederate soldiers, who were left upon the field from choice, knowing that they would be among their friends and relatives; they were cared for by the citizens and all are doing well.

Brigadier-general Williams was killed in the engagement.

Colonel Allen, of the Fourth Louisiana, was severely wounded, also Generals Breckinridge and Lovell.

Today (Wednesday) the U.S. gunboats Essex and Sumter went up some five miles to attack the C.S. gunboat Arkansas.

Two reports are current in town—one that she has been blown up by a shell from the U.S. gunboat Essex, which, it is said, reached the magazine; and the other, that she probably damaged herself, so as not to be manageable, and was blown up, to prevent her falling into the hands of the U.S. officials. Since the above was written, we learn that several wounded Confederates were taken to various hospitals in this city.

...The nerves of the inhabitants of this city have been so highly affected for the past two or three days, that every sound in the distance is translated into some message of slaughter and carnage. The female portion of the population are alike down on Feds and Confeds.

No one knows which way to turn him
All things either melt or burn

THE RAM ARKANSAS

Some doubt pervades the public mind in relation to the destruction of this far-famed boat. If she was not destroyed, our military authorities have been thoroughly deceived as to her identity. We admit that it is possible that the Confederates disguised the Music, or some other boat, and sent her down for the express purpose of practicing such a deception, in which case they were completely successful. The only doubt in our mind arises from the fact of her easy conquest, and from the manner in which she seemed to have dodged the assailants, whom it was understood she was eager to encounter. This more than her destruction, if destroyed, would militate against the renown of this new arm of national defense.

Important Order

The following important order was issued on Saturday last by the Major-General Commanding of the Department of the Gulf:

Headquarters Department of the Gulf

New Orleans, La. August 9, 1862

Special Order No. 57

Soldiers of the Army of the Gulf—Your successes have heretofore been substantially bloodless.

Taking and holding the most important strategic and commercial positions with the aid of the gallant Navy, by the wisdom of your combinations and the moral power of your arms, it has been left for the fast few days to baptize you in blood.

The Spanish conqueror of Mexico won imperishable renown by landing in that country and burning his transport ships, to cut off all hope of retreat. You, more wise and economical, but with equal providence against retreat, sent yours home.

Organized to operate on the sea coast, you advanced your outposts to Baton Rouge, the capital of the State of Louisiana, more than two hundred and fifty miles into the interior.

Attacked there by a division of our rebel enemies, under command of a Major-General recreant to loyal Kentucky, whom some of us would have honored before his apostasy, of doubly superior numbers, you have repulsed in the open field his myrmidons, who took advantage of your sickness, from the malaria of the marshes of Vicksburg to make a cowardly attack.

The brigade at Baton Rouge has routed the enemy.

He has lost three Brigadier-Generals, killed, wounded and prisoners, many colonels and field officers. He has more than a thousand killed and wounded.

You have captured three pieces of artillery, six caissons, two stands of colors, and a large number of prisoners.

You have buried his dead on the field of battle and are caring for his wounded. You have convinced him that you are never so sick as not to fight your enemy if he desires the contest.

You have shown him that if he cannot take an outpost after weeks of preparation, what would be his fate with the main body. If your General should say he was proud of you, it would only be to praise himself; but he will say he is proud to be one of you.

In this battle the Northeast and the Northwest mingled their blood on the field, as they had long ago joined their hearts, in support of the Union.

Michigan stood by Maine, Massachusetts supported Indiana, Wisconsin aided Vermont, while Connecticut, represented by the sons of the evergreen shamrock, fought as our fathers did at Boyne Waters.

While we all honor the loss of many brave comrades, we who were absent envy them the privilege of dying upon the battlefield for our country, under the starry folds of her victorious flag.

The colors and guidons of the several corps engaged in the contest will have inscribed on them "Baton Rouge".

To complete the victory, the iron-clad steamer Arkansas, the last naval hope of the rebellion, hardly awaited the gallant attack of the Essex, but followed the example of her sisters the Merrimack, the Manassas, the Mississippi, and the Louisiana by her own destruction.   Major Gen. Butler

THE FIGHT AT BATON ROUGE

FURTHER PARTICULARS

We take the following additional particulars of the recent action at Baton Rouge from yesterday's Delta:

Lieutenant Weitzel visited Baton Rouge on Wednesday. The following is his report of the engagement:

HEADQUARTERS BATON ROUGE

August 7, 1862

General – I have the honor to acknowledge the receipt of your favor of yesterday.

Your troops at this place have won a glorious victory. I do not consider that there is the least danger of an attack for the present, because one of the several reconnoitering parties sent out this morning and which has returned, reports five abandoned caissons on the Greenwell Springs road. We have sent out to bring them in. This indicates a hasty retreat on the part of the enemy. Our forces could not march a mile. The conduct of these men was magnificently glorious. The attack was undoubtedly made upon representations of rebels within our lines that our troops were nearly all sick and demoralized, and Gen. Breckinridge undoubtedly expected, in conjunction with the ram Arkansas, to make a successful dash. It was a complete failure. The ram is blown up. Their troops were repulsed.

Gen. Williams disposed his forces as follows, viz: The Fourth Wisconsin on the extreme left on the right bank of Bayou Gross, with two pieces of Manning's Battery in the Arsenal Grounds on the left bank of Bayou Gross , to sweep the grounds; on the left of the Wisconsin Fourth. The Ninth Connecticut was posted on the right of the Fourth Wisconsin, with two pieces in the rear of center, and two pieces in rear of the right. All of these pieces were of Manning's Battery, and were posted on either side of the knoll in the Government Cemetery.

Next came the Fourteenth Maine, posted in rear of the Bayou Sara road, and to the left of Greenwell Springs road.

Next came the Twenty-first Indiana, posted in the rear of Magnolia Cemetery, with four pieces of Everett's Battery, (under the command of Lieut. Carruth) on their left on the Greenwell Springs road. The Indiana Battery of two pieces came up to the support of these pieces after the battle commenced. Next came the Sixth Michigan, posted across the country road on right of the Magnolia Cemetery and across the Clay Cut road their left supporting two pieces of Everett's Battery, posted on the road on the right of the Magnolia Cemetery.

The Seventh Vermont was posted in rear of the Twenty-first Indiana and Sixth Michigan, on the right of the Catholic Cemetery. The Thirtieth Massachusetts came next, forming the right, and posted about one-half a mile in rear of the State House, supporting Nims' Battery.

This disposition of the forces was made with the supposition that the enemy would our left flank depended upon gunboat support. The only fault of disposition –perhaps rendered unavoidable by the formations of the ground—was that the camps of the Fourteenth Maine and Twenty- first Indiana were pitched in front of their position, in line of battle, and consequently came into the possession of the enemy for a short time.

The enemy formed line of battle on the open ground, bordering on the Greenwell Springs road, and attempted to draw our forces out. Failing in this, they advanced rapidly on the ground between the Clinton and Clay Cut roads. The whole brunt of the attack, consequently, fell upon the Fourteenth Maine, Twenty-first Indiana and Sixth Michigan. As soon as it became apparent that this was the real point of attack, Gen. Williams ordered up the Ninth Connecticut, Fourth Wisconsin, and one section of Manning's Battery to support the left and the Thirtieth Massachusetts and two sections of Nims' Battery to support the right.

You will, therefore, see that the disposition (with the slight exception hinted at) and the maneuvering were faultless.

The conduct of our troops was excellent. The Twenty-first Indiana particularly distinguished *itself I saw a number of the dead of the enemy today in front of the ground they occupied; but not content with the check they gave the enemy this regiment pursued him quite a distance, strewing the ground with his dead.*

The brave Gen. Williams fell in front of the Sixth Michigan, towards the close of the conflict, while giving his men a noble example of reckless and daring bravery. He was killed by a rifle-ball in the chest.

The enemy's forces consisted of two Louisiana regiments, (the Fourth and Thirtieth) two Mississippi, the Third, Fourth, Fifth, Sixth, Seventh, and Eighth Kentucky, two Tennessee, one Alabama Regiment and thirteen guns, and a large guerrilla force. Their attacking force numbered fully 6000 men. Our actual force engaged was not over 2000. Three companies of the Sixth Michigan covered themselves with glory in recovering from a large force two guns posted on the right of the Magnolia Cemetery, which temporarily were left by our forces. These same three companies captured the colors of the Fourth Louisiana, but only after they had shot down four successive color bearers.

The exact loss on our side is not yet reported. But certain it is, that it is much less than that of the enemy.

I am sir, very respectfully, your obedient servant.

G. Weitzel
Lieut. U.S. Eng. And Chief Engineer
Department of the Gulf
Major General B.F. Butler, Commanding

SOLDIERS ACCOUNT OF THE BATTLE

New Orleans, August 9, 1862 – The troops were posted as follows, from right to left: Thirtieth Regiment   Massachusetts,   Sixth   Michigan, Twenty-First   Indiana,   Seventh   Vermont, Fourteenth   Maine,   Ninth   Connecticut,   Fourth Wisconsin and   Fourth Massachusetts.   Battery posed on the left, supported by ninth Connecticut and Fourth Wisconsin; Everett's Battery Sixth Massachusetts, supported by Fourteenth Maine and   Seventh   Vermont;   Second   Massachusetts Battery, Captain Nims, supported by Twenty-First Indiana: -- Battery supported by Sixth Wisconsin and Thirtieth Massachusetts.

The   Fourteenth   Maine,   Twenty-first   Indiana and   Sixth   Wisconsin,   were   the   first   regiments engaged. They held in check about eight thousand Confederates for about one hour, when they were forced back a quarter of a mile, the Confederates occupying their camps, which they destroy Fourth Wisconsin were   not   able   to   ascertain   the   exact position of the enemy and were of but very little service   until   the   new   line   was   formed).   Capt. Nims, Capt Everett and the battery on the right and two pieces of the Fourth Massachusetts on the extreme left, opened a murderous fire from their batteries, which was returned with spirit by the Confederates. The battle raged without a moment's intermission and with great severity for two hours. During this time nothing but a continual roar of artillery, the rattle of musketry, the shouts of the combatants, and the groans of the wounded and dying, was to be heard. Capt. Nim's Battery was compelled to fall back, his guns being so hot it was impossible to use them. He took his position on the left of the Twenty-first Indiana and ordered water to be brought to cool his guns. While thus engaged three regiments of the Confederates charged the Twenty-first Indiana and one regiment charged Capt. Nims. Gen Williams, perceiving the perilous position of the regiment and knowing the consequences of having the center broken, took his position at the head of the loading rifles) and allowed the Confederates to approach with a few rods. General Williams than gave the command, "Forward! Double-quick!" and with a deafening cheer they rushed to the charge. The shock of two such masses advancing shook the entire field.

The struggle was fierce and the killed and wounded on both sides numerous. General Williams fell, shot through he heart. This was the signal for a general onset on both sides. Capt Nims lost two of his guns, but charged with his sabers and revolvers and retook them. The Twenty-First regiment repulsed three times their own number, and drove them back in confusion. I was at this time detached with the first platoon of our company (Fourth regiment Wisconsin) to skirmish on the extreme left of the line, to prevent a surprise on our flank. I took a position one mile outside the old picket lines, in true Yankee style—behind stump and trees. The rebels did not think it safe to honor us with a shot. We were fired at, however, by some of our pickets, who were driven in from the front, they mistaking us for rebels. They also reported us to the gunboat Essex as rebels, and she commenced shelling our lines. In riding in to correct the mistake, a shell burst directly behind me; my horse taking fright, I broke my stirrup, and fell heavily to the ground, and consequently was obliged to retire from the field.

The rebels were forced back one mile land a half our forces occupying their original position. Our men lay on their arms during the day and night.

The Confederate loss was heavy in killed and wounded. Our loss was about 200 killed and wounded. Among them were several distinguished officers, whose names I did not learn.

On visiting a portion of the field on the morning of the 6th, I counted sixty-four Confederate soldiers and a Colonel that were not yet buried, some twenty hours after the engagement. Prisoners taken report their force at from 6000 to 10,000 while our force did not exceed 2500.

The field officers of the Fourth Wisconsin Regiment showed great personal bravery. Lieut.. Colonel J. A. Beene, acting Colonel, retained his position at the head of his regiment during the entire battle.

While standing with one hand on a fence, in a perfect shower of grape, a cannon ball passed between him and the fence, and under his arm, but he did not change his position.

G. W. Porter
Corporal Fourth Wisconsin Regiment

OUR OWN ACCOUNT

(CORRESPONDENCE OF THE NEW ORLEANS DELTA)

Baton Rouge, La.   August 7, 1862

My Dear Captain Clark—Though just from the field of battle, I cannot say that the smoke or glory can attach itself to my skirts; for, though no matter what my fighting propensities may be, it was not my good fortune either to take part in the repulse of the Camp Moore army, or in the destruction of the Arkansas. The latter, I will dispose of a l'outrance, by asserting that it was a fair stand-up, knock-down and scratch-gravel fight between the two iron-clad nondescripts—the Union Essex and the Rebel Arkansas. No matter what the rebels may say, it was a square fight. The Arkansas took the position of her choice, in a deep bend of the river, where she tied up, but with her starboard and port broadsides sweeping the river up and down, and her bow raking across, at the same time, ready to dash across and plunge her bow into any vessel attempting to pass in front of her. Porter, of the Essex with a seaman's instinct, saw this plan of the enemy, and wisely laid below, but not more than three hundred yards distant, whence she pounded solid nine-inch shot into the Arkansas, till, a favorable breach being made in her bow just under her ports, an incendiary shell was exploded in the breach, instantly setting the Arkansas on fire. Her bow, where the shell burst, being the windward end, in a few minutes the navy who were so fortunate as to be present at this last naval combat of two iron-clads, had the satisfaction of seeing the crew of the rebel scuttling on shore, while the flames were bursting out on every side. but be it understood and recorded, all this time the Arkansas was fighting her battery, till her fast burning off, she floated into the middle of the river, where in a little while she blew up. Let no credulous or unbelieving rebel flatter his soul that this was not the Arkansas that was sunk and destroyed. So much for the naval part of the affair—important, as enabling the gunboats to act without impediment with the land forces.

The battle of Baton Rouge may be characterized as one of the most soldier-like, skillfully planned fights of this war. Gen. Williams, with his well-known abilities as a leader, scorned to rally behind houses and fences, and taking in with one glance the plan of the enemy's attack, made all his preparations to resist and oppose them.

Two highways run out of Baton Rouge—one above and one below on each side of the town; about a mile and a half of road cuts these two roads at right angles, while extending from road to road is a large cemetery, facing towards the city and looking directly into the camps of the Indiana, Massachusetts, and Connecticut regiments. The front of this cemetery is fenced with paling, while the cemetery is thickly strewn with large tombs and overgrown with high rank weeds. This was the position of the Rebel centre. Our centre was composed of the Indiana Twenty-First, the Massachusetts and Connecticut, drawn up on the opposite side of the roads, and not more than forty-five rods distant. The rebel right approached, through corn fields and over a rolling country, attacked with great impetuosity the Fourteenth Maine's camp and drove them out, burning and pillaging the camp in a few minutes. The Fourteenth Maine rallied and supported by the Massachusetts and Nims' Battery returned to the attack and drove the enemy back with great slaughter. The fiercest part of the conflict at this tide of the battle occurred before and within a house which the rebels obstinately determined to get possession of. The most conspicuous of the rebels at this place was a huge negro, armed and equipped with knapsack, musket and uniform; he led the rebels, and met his death at the hands of one of our men. Pressed back by our left, and our ground regained, the battle raged in front with desperate fierceness.

So silently did the rebels approach and so well were they concealed, that they were in the cemetery and drawn up in battle array, without our knowing it. With a yell they rushed up to the fence, dashed through it and across the road, bearing everything before them. At one time the opposing forces were hand to hand, and our handful of men were driven out of their camps and back into the town: but rallied on every hand by their officers, and the cool daring of Gen. Williams, assisted by the gunboats that began to fire shell on each flank with perfect accuracy and deadly effect, our troops bravely rushed to the front and down the entire rebel center, back across the road into and beyond the cemetery, from which they were not able again to emerge.

Four times they made desperate efforts to come out from behind the tombs and cross the road, but each time they were driven back, until, finally, they were in full panic retreat. Our own men were too much exhausted to pursue. On our right, in the meantime, the rebels, under Gen. Clarke, made a desperate effort to flank us and get in our rear. It was here that the admirable generalship of Williams displayed itself. Anticipating this very movement he had placed Manning's battery of six pieces supported by the Wisconsin and Vermont regiments, while the Michigan regiment was strongly posted at the crossing of the roads, and commanding the entire approach of the enemy's left. Here the battle raged fiercely, and after the rebels' flank movement was repulsed and driven back not to return—here it was that the gallant General fell at the head of the Indiana and Michigan regiments; but not before victory had lighted up that fine manly face with its glow of triumph. I am convinced that had Williams not fallen, he would have destroyed the whole of the rebel forces.

By 10 A.M. all firing had ceased, and the enemy had retired with haste, and left over 300 dead on the field of battle. Every one of his dead was buried by our men, except many who died in the retreat, or were killed by the long-reaching shells of our gunboats. The field presented evidences of the desperation of the combat at the crossing of the roads where the rebels had endeavored to flank us, and where they were met by the Indiana and Michigan Regiments. The men fought hard. Those who had lost their arms tore up the rains from the fences. More than one rebel was found dead who had been killed in this way. In one spot behind a beautiful tomb, with effigies of infant children kneeling, twelve dead rebels were found in one heap. Everywhere they strewed the earth, and made ghastly the quiet graveyard under which they soon lay—victims to a madness which if much longer persisted in, will make the entire land red with blood; for the rebellion must be crushed, if we have to use the last, most certain, but most fatal weapon left to us. Let us pray that they will not force us to this last dread alternative—that they will return to reason in time, and dismiss the bitter hatred which they nourish in their hearts against us. Let them remember that as "love begets love," so does scorn and hatred beget their like; and let them be assured that it will be a sorry day for Southern homes when the fierce fires of rage and hate begin to burn in the Northern heart. I am convinced that, as yet, there is little of that feeling existing; but it will come.

To return to our feeble account of this battle. The enemy repulsed; their short-lived Arkansas blown to atoms—in retreat and discomfiture they have returned to Camp Moore –ay, this time these who have been practicing guerrilla warfare and assassinating defenceless, wounded soldiers, have been punished. The inhabitants of certain villages who sit listless on the levee as a man-of-war passes up or down, spring into life, and bring out the murderous double shot gun to fire up on the hospital ships—these gentry will find that they can be made to suffer and feel. Our gallant army at Baton Rouge, in their first battle, have behaved *like veterans. Let us praise the living and mourn the dead, and cry, "Long Live the Republic!" Death to traitors and aristocrats! Death to the man who stabs our common mother—the Union!" If she must die, let us all die with her—let not a man, woman or child live after her.   Webster*

THE BUTLER CENSURE DOCUMENTS

General Orders, Headquarters Department of the Gulf

No. 62 1/2. New Orleans, August 25th, 1862.

The commanding general has carefully revised the official reports of the action of August 5th at Baton Rouge, to collect the evidence of the gallant deeds and meritorious services of those engaged in that brilliant victory. The name of the lamented and gallant General Williams has already passed into history. Colonel Roberts of the Seventh Vermont volunteers, fell mortally wounded while rallying his men. He was worthy of a better disciplined regiment and a better fate. Glorious as it is to die for one's country, yet his regiment gave him the inexpressible pain of seeing it break in confusion when not pressed by the enemy and refuse to march to the aid of the outnumbered and almost overwhelmed Indianians. The Seventh Vermont regiment, by a fatal mistake, had already fired into the same regiment they had refused to support, killed and wounding several. The commanding general therefore excepts the Seventh Vermont from General Orders No. 57, and will not permit their colors to be inscribed with a name which could bring to its officers and men no proud thought. It is further ordered that the colors of that regiment be not borne by them until such time as they shall have earned the right to them, and the earliest opportunity will be given this regiment, to show whether they are worthy descendants of those who fought beside Allen and with Starke at Bennington. The following have honorable mention. * * * John Donoghue, Fourth Massachusetts battery, who brought off from the camp of the Seventh Vermont regiment their colors at the time of their retreat. * * *

By command of Major-General Butler.
WM. H. WEIGEL,
First Lieutenant and Acting Assistant Adjutant-General.

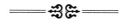

General Lorenzo Thomas, Adjutant General, Washington, D. C.:

In justice to the regiment which I have the honor to command, the Seventh regiment of Vermont Volunteers, I find myself under necessity of calling for an examination into the statements made by the major-general commanding the department in Order No. 62 ½, dates August 25th, 1862, which are calculated, in my opinion, to bring unmerited disgrace upon the regiment and the State from which it comes. I respectfully request that a court of inquiry may be assembled as soon as convenient to investigate and report upon the battle of Baton Rouge and the part taken in that engagement by my regiment, with the view that justice may be done to it and the service. Regretting exceedingly to find myself impelled to ask for the scrutiny of a victory which should fill all generous hearts only with gratitude and pride,

I have the honor to be, sir, very respectfully, your obedient servant,

W. C. HOLBROOK,
Major, Commanding Seventh Regiment Vermont Volunteers.

Camp Parapet, La., September 2d, 1862.

It is much to be regretted that a regiment in this quarter should be compelled to defend itself against unmerited dishonor from its commanding general as well as against the enemy and extraordinary exposure and disease; but I concur with Major Holbrook in the necessity of an investigation into the facts connected with the battle of Baton Rouge by a court of inquiry, with the view of doing justice to the Seventh Vermont Volunteers and to the service.

J. W. PHELPS,
Brigadier-General.

Headquarters Department of the Gulf,
New Orleans, La., September 14th, 1862.
Brigadier-General Thomas, Adjutant-General

General: I enclose the somewhat anomalous application of Major Holbrook, commanding the

Seventh regiment Vermont volunteers, with a copy of the general order complained about. It will be seen that I only give the result of official reports, so that I do not feel personally touched by the matter or manner of the communication. Of the conduct of Major Holbrook there is no complaint; being field officer of the day, of the post, he was not in the action. If consistent with the rules of the service to inquire into the resume by the commanding general of the events of an action, I should be glad to have it done. For if the regiment has been unjustly treated it could give no one more pleasure than myself to see it righted. As there has been some rivalry of feeling I do not think it would be best to detail a court from the officers of the regiments at Baton Rouge. I may further say that I suggested to Major Holbrook that he might select his court of inquiry from any of the officers here not of that brigade.

BENJ. F. BUTLER,
Major-General, Commanding.
Washington, October 3d, 1862.
Maj.-General Benjamin F. Butler, New Orleans

General: Your letter of September 14th, inclosing the application of Major W. C. Holbrook for a court of inquiry on the conduct of the Seventh Vermont Volunteers at the battle of Baton Rouge , has been received and referred to the Secretary of War. No officer can at this time be sent to new

Orleans to constitute such a court. The course suggested by you in regard to the proposed investigation seems unobjectionable in all respects. You have full authority to adopt it.

H. W. Halleck,
General-in-Chief.
Headquarters Department of the Gulf,

Hon. E. M. Stanton:

I wrote you a few weeks since of the charges of General Butler in his order No. 62 ½, against the Seventh Vermont regiment in the battle at Baton Rouge. These charges are believed to be grossly unjust, and have stirred up the people of Vermont. Nothing short of an entirely impartial court of inquiry, to be appointed at and sent on from Washington, will satisfy our people. They are brave, loyal and patriotic to the core, and for that very reason will not quietly sit down under charges which reflect upon the State. May I have assurances that action will be taken at Washington?

—=❧ॐ☙=—

Frederick Holbrook,
Governor of Vermont.

The Legislature of Vermont :

Resolved, That His Excellency, the Governor, be requested to demand an investigation by the War Department at Washington of all the circumstances relating to the conduct of the Seventh Vermont regiment at the battle of Baton Rouge. And be it further

Resolved, That if it appears that the charges against said regiment for cowardice and unsoldier-like conduct are false, that the governor be requested to demand the immediate transfer of the Seventh regiment to some other department of the United States service.

Whereas, Charges of misconduct have been made by the general commanding the Department of the Gulf against the Seventh regiment Vermont Volunteers. And

Whereas, It is due to the honor and dignity of the State that such charges be fully investigated, in order that any injustice therein may be publicly declared, therefore,

Resolved, By the Senate and House of Representatives, that the governor be requested to demand of the President of the United States, as an act of justice to said regiment and to the State of Vermont, that a board of inquiry be appointed to hear and determine such charges as soon as may be, according to the usual course of military inquery.

BOARD OF INQUIRY
DEPARTMENT OF THE GULF,

City of New Orleans, October 23, 1862.

Pursuant to special orders from department headquarters, viz:
SPECIAL ORDERS, HEADQUARTERS DEPARTENT OF THE GULF
No. 462. New Orleans, October 21, 1862

A board of inquiry, consisting of the following officers: Col. H. C. Deming, president; Col. J. W. Turner, Lieut. Col. A. B. Farr, Lieut. W. L. G. Greene, recorder, is ordered to examine and report upon the facts and circumstances relative to the condition as to discipline and efficiency of the Seventh Regiment Vermont Volunteers at the time of the battle of Baton Rouge and the conduct of the officers and men in that action.

By order of Major-General Butler;
R. S. Davis,
Captain and Acting Assistant Adjutant General.

DEPARTMENT OF THE GULF,
New Orleans, November 3, 1862.

The board met pursuant to adjournment. Present, all the members. The board, having fully weighed and considered the evidence, report as follows: It appears from the evidence that when the Seventh Regiment Vermont Volunteers was called upon to participate in the battle of Baton Rouge it had been very much reduced in numbers and doubtless in morale by the severities of the campaign at Vicksburg and by long confinement on board transports. On the morning of the battle the regiment had present for duty about 250 men, about 520 men sick, of whom 200 were in hospital. About 225 men were in line early in the action. The commanding officer of the regiment, Colonel Roberts, fell under the sharpest volley that was fired that day, and shortly after his fall the regiment fled about 100 feet to the rear and to the cover of some gullies in a disorderly manner. About two-fifths of the men present for duty did not return to the position in line of battle during the day. It appears that early in the action Lieutenant-Colonel Fullam had been dispatched by his colonel to see to the firing of a battery which was endangering the regiment; that Major Holbrook was officer of the day. Upon the fall of the colonel, therefore, the command of the regiment devolved temporarily upon Captain (now Major) Porter, who seems to have behaved creditably in a trying position. When the lieutenant colonel returned he assumed command of the regiment. The only testimony before the board discreditable to him is the following, from Lieutenant-Colonel Elliott's deposition: I did see something in the conduct of officers which I thought deserving of censure. I saw Colonel Fullam, after they had fallen back, seeking protection, drawing his regiment up in a ravine. I asked what he was doing there. He said he was getting his men into a sheltered position. I saw no other officers show a disposition to evade duty. I think the regiment was over 200 yards in the rear of their camp.

So far as any evidence appears it would seem that the line officers behaved well during the day. It appears that the Seventh Vermont Regiment, or a part of it, did fire into the Twenty-first Indiana, but there is an exculpation to be found in the testimony of the commanding officer of the Indiana regiment, Captain Grimsley, to wit: Occupying the position they did the Seventh had no means of knowing where we were. * * * My impression is that when we received the volleys from the Seventh Vermont we ran under a fire which was already going on. It appears also from the testimony of various witnesses that the field was covered by dense fog and smoke, so that it was quite impossible to distinguish a friend from a foe at the distance the two regiments were apart; and, moreover, that the position of the Indiana regiment was very frequently changed. It does not appear that any orders were communicated to the Vermont regiment during the day which they disobeyed. It appears that the colors of the regiment were retained by the color guard during the action, and were brought off the field by the guard when the regiment fell back. It appears that the camp colors alleged by Captain Manning, of the Fourth Massachusetts Battery, to have been brought from the camp of the Seventh Vermont by John Donoghue were two markers of the form in common use and one small United States flag, which had been used for no military purpose for a long time previously.

HENRY C. DEMING,
Colonel Twelfth Regt. Conn. Vols., President of the Court.

JNO. W. TURNER,
Colonel and C. S.

A. B. FARR,
Lieutenant-Colonel   Twenty-sixth   Regiment Massachusetts Vols.,

WILLIAM L. G. GREENE,
Lieutenant   Second   Louisiana   Volunteers, Recorder.

HEADQUARTERS   DEPARTMENT   OF   THE GULF,
New Orleans, November 6, 1862.

The commanding general has examined with care the findings, proceedings, and testimony of the court of inquiry, whereof Col. Henry C. Deming is president, in the matter of the Seventh Regiment

Vermont Volunteers, and approves the proceedings and findings. It is apparent that every conclusion arrived at by the court is supported by the testimony of the witnesses called on behalf of the regiment. The general is constrained to find that the charge against the regiment of breaking in disorder before the enemy is fully proved. Two-fifths of the regiment never returned to the line of battle after they broke and fled; that the regiment did fire upon the Indiana regiment, and that that was the only firing done by the regiment that day, although they held the center of the line, which was most hotly pressed. The general is glad to find that most of the line officers behaved well, and that the official reports which led him to believe that the regimental colors were lost by the regiment were mistakes, and therefore he has pleasure in ordering the colors of the regiment to be restored to the regiment with privilege to carry them, but he cannot order them to be inscribed with the name of the glorious battle of Baton Rouge. The general doubts not that now, having an officer as commander who will not form them out of sight for shelter in a ravine during an action as did their late lieutenant colonel, the regiment will in its next action retrieve its position and earn a proud name for itself and State.

BENJ. F. BUTLER
Major-General, Commanding

—— ⚜ ——

General Orders, HDQRS. DEPARTMENT OF THE GULF,
No. 98. New Orleans, November 20, 1862.

The commanding general, upon the finding of the board of inquiry upon the conduct of the Seventh Regiment Vermont Volunteers at the battle of Baton Rouge, learns that he was led into a mistake by the official reports of that action as to the loss by that regiment of its colors, it proving to have been the camp color left in camp and not the regimental color that was brought off the field by the Massachusetts battery. He therefore has pleasure in ordering the regimental colors to be restored to the regiment, not doubting that it will in its next action earn for itself a position and name which will be a credit to itself, its State, and country.

By command of Major-General Butler,
GEO. C. STRONG,
Assistant Adjutant-General and Chief of Staff.

Re-enlistment Paper

Town Bonus Letter

Mr. Proctor Swallow

Dear Sir

The Town of Poultney have voted a bounty of $200 additional to what you have already received. The Town requires an affidavit that you have not sold out your claim for bounty.

I enclose an affidavit for you to Sign and Swear before some person authorized to administer oaths.

You can send the affidavit to me and I will draw the bounty and do with it as you direct - - either send it to you, or keep it here, until your return or pay it to whom you wish.

Please send as soon as you can - - before the Town rescind their Vote.

Truly Yours

J.B Beaman
Poultney
March 13, 1865

If there are any others re-enlisted men from Poutney or <u>credited</u> to Poutney – have them make similar affidavits –and send on---and I will draw their pay.   J.B.B.

BIBLIOGRAPHY

BOOKS –ONE AUTHOR

Benedict, G.C., *Vermont in the Civil War: Volume 2.* Burlington, Vermont: Free Press Association. 1886. (p. 1-79)

Catton, Bruce, *A Stillness at Appomattox. Garden City, New York: Doubleday & Company,* 1954.
>   *This Hallowed Ground.* New York: Doubleday & Company, 1956.

Coffin, Howard, *Full Duty: Vermonters in the Civil War.* Woodstock, Vermont: Countryman Press Inc., 1993.

Davis, William C., *Commanders of the Civil War: Rebels & Yankees.* New York: Salamander Books Ltd., 1990.

Denney, Robert E., *Civil War Years: A Day-by-Day Chronicle of the Life of a Nation.*

New York: Sterling Publishing Co. Inc., 1992.

Foote, Shelby. *Fort Sumter to Perryville.* New York: Random House, 1958.
>   *Red River to Appomattox.* New York: Random House, 1974.

Holbrook, William C., *A Narrative of the Services of the Officers and Enlisted Men of the 7ᵗʰ*

Regiment of Vermont Volunteers. New York: American Bank Note Co., 1882.

Jordan, Robert Paul, *The Civil War.* Washington DC: National Geographic Society, 1969.

MacPherson, James, *Battle Cry of Freedom..* New York: Oxford University Press, 1988.

Pullen, John J., *The Twentieth Maine: A Volunteer Regiment in the Civil War.* Philadelphia: Lippincott. 1957.

BOOKS-TWO AUTHORS

Sherman, Michael, Sessions, Gene, Potash P. Jeffrey. *Freedom and Unity: A History of Vermont.* Barre, Vermont: Vermont Historical Society, 2004.

Smith, Barbara Bentley and Baker, Nina Bentley editors. *Burning Rails as We Pleased: The Civil War Letters of William Garrigues Bentley, 104th Ohio Volunteer Regiment.* Jefferson, North Carolina: McFarland & Company, Inc., 2003.

ENCYCLOPEDIA ARTICLE

Worcester. Donald E., "Maximilian", The World Book Encyclopedia, 1967 ed., vol. 13, p.252.

NEWSPAPER ARTICLES

Baton Rouge Daily News August 7, 1862.

*Rutland Daily Herald, 1861 –1865 (selected issues).*Castleton College, Castleton, Vermont.

INTERVIEWS

Fenton, Anna.   Interview by Kenena   Spalding, Spa-Whit-Ton   Farm,   Middletown   Springs, Vermont.   September 2003.

DOCUMENTS

Swallow, Proctor.   Civil War Letters.   Collection of the Spalding Family.

A   Declaration   for   Invalid   Pension. Washington   DC: National Archives.

Notarized   Sworn   Deposition   given   on June 5, 1866. Washington DC: National Archives.

Pension Files containing support letters for his claims. Washington DC: National Archives.

Military records. Washington DC: National Archives.

MAPS

Gorlinski, Joseph, *Topographical Plan of the City and Battle Field of Baton Rouge, LA. Fought on the 5th of August 1862.* Office of the Chief of Engineers U.S. Army.

Historical War Map 1862 by Asher & Co. Geographical and Map Division, Washington DC: Library of Congress. (only a portion of the map used)

Siege Operations at Spanish Fort, Mobile Bay, by the U.S. Forces under Maj. Gen. E.R. Canby. Geographical and Map Division, Washington DC: Library of Congress.

Texas Coast showing Points of Occupation of Expedition under Maj. Gen. N.P. Banks, November 1863. Geographical and Map Division, Washington DC: Library of Congress.

PHOTOGRAPHS

Fort Barrancas Redoubt. Washington DC: National Archives.

Seventh Vermont Regiment Home Again. Montpelier, Vermont: Vermont Historical Society.

References

[1]   State authorities intended that this regiment be sent to join other Vermont regiments with the Army of the Potomac in Virginia. Another act of the legislature on November 12, 1861 had authorized the Governor to recruit a regiment to be attached to the New England Division that the Secretary of War had authorized General Ben Butler to organize and which would be armed and equipped at the expense of the United States. This became the Eighth Vermont.   General Butler sought to have both regiments assigned to him and visited Montpelier personally. When the State denied his request, he went to the War Department and obtained the result he wanted. The original equipment of the Eighth Vermont was marked with the initials N.E.D indicating it belonged to the New England Division. The equipment of the Seventh Vermont was never marked in this way.   (Holbrook)

[2]   Col. Roberts served as a lieutenant in the First Vermont Regiment. His ability was noted by Gen. Phelps and he recommended him for command of the Seventh.

[3]   Col. Phelps, a West Point graduate, had commanded the First Vermont Regiment in the Battle of Big Bethel. When their three-month enlistment expired in the fall, many of the men who served with him joined the Seventh Vermont Regiment.

4   *Rutland Daily Herald,* January 27, 1862.

5   (Holbrook, 3, 4).

6   Days later when a bad storm struck, their decision proved to be a wise one.

7   When Phelps was in Virginia with the First Vermont his talents were recognized and he was promoted to brigadier general. He was ordered to New Orleans to become part of the expedition against the city. He and Gen. Butler knew each other at Fort Monroe. (Holbrook 6).

8   (Holbrook 10-16)

9   General Willliams sought to toughen the men. He continued this practice even as they were exhausted from digging the canal. They considered him a martinet.

10 The assistant engineer on the steamer *Whitman* was found to be a rebel with plans to blow-up the ship. Repairs were made and he was taken off board.

11 General Williams ordered the burning in retribution and as a warning to other towns along the river not to fire upon the soldiers.

12 Lorenzo Brooks commanded F Company. The *Ceres* was heavily shelled by Rebel artillery returning from a night mission; he was killed instantly by the second shot.

[13] It read in part: "The commanding general has carefully reviewed the official reports of the action of August 5th at Baton Rouge, to collect the evidence of the gallant deeds and meritorious services of those engaged in that brilliant victory. The name of the lamented and gallant General Williams has already passed into history. Colonel Roberts of the Seventh Vermont volunteers, fell mortally wounded rallying his men. He was worthy of a better disciplined regiment and a better fate. Glorious as it is to die for one's country, yet his regiment gave him the inexpressible pain of seeing it break in confusion when not pressed by the enemy and refuse to march to the aid of the outnumbered and almost overwhelmed Indianians. The Seventh Vermont regiment, by a fatal mistake, had already fired into the same regiment they had refused to support, killing and wounding several. The commanding general therefore excepts the Seventh Vermont from General Orders No. 57, and will not therefore permit their colors to be inscribed with a name (the Battle of Baton Rouge) which could bring to its officers and men no proud thought. It is further ordered that the colors of the regiment be not borne by them until such time as they shall have earned the right to them, and the earliest opportunity will be given this regiment to show whether they are worthy descendants of those who fought beside Allen and with Starke at Bennington." See Appendix for more details on this brouhaha.

14   Phelps reasoned that because many of the White Union troops were dying from disease and thus weakening his forces, the arming of the free blacks provided a way to overcome this deficiency.

15   On the same date, the Confederate War Department issued General Order No. 63 designating Phelps an outlaw and that should he be captured he would "not be regarded as become a prisoner of war, but held in close confinement for execution as a felon at such time and place as the President (Jefferson Davis) shall order."

16   (Holbrook 22-27).

17   Captain Ruggles was popular with the men and they grieved his death from sunstroke on July 24, 1862.

18   Fanny was his sister and the wife of Loomis.

19   The *Whitman* was not a lucky ship. On the way down the Mississippi River with a number of sick and wounded Union soldiers aboard, she caught fire and sank. It was the same ship the Rebel engineer had tried to sabotage earlier.

20   Grove Scribner was fighting with the Army of the Potomac. He qualified as a sharpshooter and joined the 2nd U.S. Sharpshooters on Dec. 31, 1861. He participated in all the major battles of the Virginia theatre. He was wounded

on the skirmish line in1864 fighting in the wilderness with Grant at Spotsylvania.

21 The child was Fred Whitcomb Spalding, the grandfather of Fanny and Helen Spalding who preserved and passed on these letters.

22 (Holbrook 47).

23 (Holbrook 50).

24 The premature discharge of an eight inch seacoast howitzer while a detachment from Company I was servicing the gun was caused by the carelessness of the corporal in charge of the detail whose duty it was to properly thumb the vent. This he did not do and his negligence cost him the middle finger of his right hand. Private Robert Ripley had is right arm blown off and died within a few days. Private James B. Royce was blown into the air and his arm later amputated near the shoulder.

25 (Holbrook 50,52).

26 No system of automatic replacements for existing units existed in most states. The only way a regiment could get more soldiers was to send a recruiting party home to enlist new men.

27 (Holbrook 58,59,61).

28 On October 19, 1864 a group of Confederates made a daring raid upon the town of St. Albans and robbed three banks of over $200,000 and fled back across the Canadian border.

29 A new son had joined the family of Loomis and Fanny on September 29, 1864.

30 Fannie Stevens became his wife after the war. She is not to be confused with his sister Fanny Spalding. She may have been the sister of Ursula Stevens who he mentioned often in letters before the furlough, but not afterwards.

31 Uncle Proc must have made friends with his two-year old nephew while on furlough.

32 (Holbrook 64-67).

33 General Weitzel had accepted the surrender of the city of Richmond on April 3.

34 *World Book,* Vol. 13, pp. 252.

35 (Holbrook 76, 77).

36 In his history of the regiment, Col. Holbrook noted that its percentage of loss by death exceeded "that of any other Vermont Regiment. Of its original members, one in every three found graves in the far South. Of the total number of deaths, 375 were from disease (not including those who died in Confederate prisons), a number far exceeding the losses of any other Vermont regiment from similar

causes. Most of the deaths occurred in the Vicksburg campaign."

[36] Helen Spalding Best, granddaughter of Loomis Spalding.

[37] Anna Whitcomb Fenton.

About The Author

Kenena Hansen Spalding is a retired teacher. She enjoys history and became a Civil War buff while her husband was stationed with the U.S. Army in Georgia. She began transcribing the letters which had been passed down through four family generations to share with her children and grandchildren. As the personality of Proctor Swallow emerged from the pages it sparked a curiosity to know more about the units and events in which he participated and this led to further research. She lives in Springfield, Virginia and is currently working on collections of other family letters.

Printed in the United States
52912LVS00001B/16-33

9 781425 919597